Cupcakes

Betty Saw

Marshall Cavendish
Cuisine

Dedication

To Choobs with Love

The publisher wishes to thank Remix Home Shoppe Sdn Bhd, for the loan of utensils for the photography of this cookbook.

Photographer : Rory Daniel
Designer   : Lynn Chin Nyuk Ling

First published as Tempt: Cupcakes to Excite, 2005
This new edition 2009

Published by Marshall Cavendish Cuisine
An imprint of Marshall Cavendish International
1 New Industrial Road, Singapore 536196

Other Marshall Cavendish Offices:

Marshall Cavendish Ltd. 5th Floor, 32-38 Saffron Hill, London EC1N 8FH, UK • Marshall Cavendish Corporation. 99 White Plains Road, Tarrytown NY 10591-9001, USA • Marshall Cavendish International (Thailand) Co Ltd. 253 Asoke, 12th Flr, Sukhumvit 21 Road, Klongtoey Nua, Wattana, Bangkok 10110, Thailand • Marshall Cavendish (Malaysia) Sdn Bhd, Times Subang, Lot 46, Subang Hi-Tech Industrial Park, Batu Tiga, 40000 Shah Alam, Selangor Darul Ehsan, Malaysia

Marshall Cavendish is a trademark of Times Publishing Limited

National Library Board Singapore Cataloguing in Publication Data

Saw, Betty.
Cupcakes / Betty Saw. – Singapore : Marshall Cavendish Cuisine, 2009.
p. cm.
ISBN-13 : 978-981-261-788-0
ISBN-10 : 981-261-788-4

1. Cupcakes. 2. Cake. I. Title.

TX771
641.8653 -- dc22   OCN304042365

Printed in Singapore by Times Printers Pte Ltd

Contents

Preface

My passion is baking cakes and I love to try all sorts of recipes and variations to come up with new cakes. But with only my husband and me at home nowadays, I find baking cakes a problem. We take days to finish eating a cake. Storage is a problem and the unfinished cake clutters up the refrigerator. The cake looks messy after it has been cut several times. It becomes dry and taste deteriorates as the days go by. When entertaining, I love to present a wide variety of desserts. However, I shudder to look at the cakes after my guests have gone through them. Those who wish to try everything will be attempting to cut small pieces and making a mess of the cakes.

I have therefore taken to baking cupcakes. They are easier to make and decorate, They can be neatly stored in the refrigerator or frozen and a few taken out each time when required. The taste is preserved and there are no more messy pieces. Cupcakes are ideal to have when entertaining because they are such dainty lovely cakes. I can also bake many more varieties and the best part is that my guests can easily pack home the remaining cakes after the party.

In fact, the first cake I learnt to bake was a cupcake in the Domestic Science class in school. It was the Queen Cupcake, which is a reduced version of the classic Pound Cake. Imperial measures were used then and the Pound Cake is a butter cake made from 1 lb of each of the main ingredients. After the Queen Cupcake, we were taught how to make the Butterfly Cake. It was a follow-on from the Queen Cupcake where we were first exposed to cream. The centre of the Queen Cupcake was hollowed out and the cutout piece cut into two wing shapes. Jam and cream were then put into the centre of the cake and the wing shapes stuck into it to make it look like a butterfly. Simple though it may seem, the Butterfly Cake is timeless and has never failed to delight my family and friends.

I invited my editor to lunch where I made cupcakes for dessert. She was so impressed that she insisted that I write a book to share my recipes with my readers. She was certain that most people today face the same problems and would benefit from these recipes. I have developed recipes to suit all tastes and they have gone through numerous rounds of testing by my close friends to get their approval before the final selection. These cakes have been such a hit with my friends that I keep receiving hints on when I am going to make these cakes for them again.

I hope you will have many hours of enjoyment in baking and eating these little cakes and cupcakes.

Cheese Cupcakes

Apple Cheesecake with Nutty Caramel Topping   *15*

Cheese Cupcake   *16*

Lemon Coconut Cheesecake   *18*

Chocolate Cheese Cupcake   *19*

Ginger Cheese Cupcake   *20*

Lychee Cheese Cupcake   *23*

Lemon Cream Cheese Cupcake   *24*

Apple Cheesecake with Nutty Caramel Topping

A delightful apple and spice cheesecake with a crunchy topping. Ideal to serve for tea or as a dessert.

Biscuit crumbs	**40 g, either ginger or digestive biscuits**
Cream cheese	**250 g, at room temperature**
Castor sugar	**90 g**
Cinnamon powder	**$^1/_4$ tsp**
Nutmeg powder	**$^1/_4$ tsp**
Canned apple sauce	**225 g**
Lemon juice	**1 Tbsp**
Eggs	**2, large (70–75 g each)**

Topping

Butter	**30 g, at room temperature**
Water	**1 Tbsp**
Brown sugar	**50 g**
Seedless dates	**15 g, chopped**
Red glace cherries	**3**
Walnuts	**30 g, toasted and chopped**
Rice crispies	**30 g**
Lemon juice	**$^1/_2$ Tbsp**
Large paper cases	**11 (5 cm base x 4 cm height)**

Line muffin pans with paper cases. Sprinkle biscuit crumbs, dividing evenly, into paper cases.

Cream the cheese, sugar and spices until smooth and fluffy. Beat in apple sauce and lemon juice. Beat in eggs until combined.

Pour cheese filling into paper cases, dividing evenly.

Bake in preheated oven at 190°C for 25 minutes. Switch off the oven, leave oven door slightly ajar and let cakes sit for 10 minutes before removing from oven.

Leave cheese cupcakes to cool in the pan.

Meanwhile, make topping by heating butter, water and brown sugar until butter melts. Stir in remaining ingredients.

Spoon the topping over each cupcake to cover completely. Chill until ready to serve.

Makes 11 cupcakes

Note: Cream cheese is an unripened cheese. It is cow's milk cheese made from single or double cream. It is smooth, buttery and creamy. Store the cheese in the refrigerator.

Cheese Cupcake

A savoury cheesecake that is a refreshing treat at any time of the day.

Self-raising flour	**110 g**
Baking powder	**2 tsp**
Butter	**110 g, diced small**
Castor sugar	**100 g**
Eggs	**2, large (70 g each), beaten with a fork**
Cheddar cheese	**50 g, finely grated**
Milk	**1 dsp**
Topping	
Parmesan cheese for sprinkling	**40 g, grated**
Medium paper cases	**17 (4.5 cm base x 2.5 cm height)**

Sift self-raising flour and baking powder together.

Cream butter and sugar for 2 minutes. Add eggs and sifted dry ingredients. Turn electric mixer on medium speed for 2 minutes. Beat in grated cheese and milk.

Using a medium-sized ice-cream scoop, place a scoop of batter in the centre of each of the paper cases.

Sprinkle top with grated Parmesan cheese.

Bake in preheated oven at 175°C (hot air) for 20 minutes or until topping is golden.

Makes 17 cupcakes

Note: Cheddar is a popular cheese with a unique 'nutty' flavour. To grate a small amount for use, cut the required amount of cheddar from the block into small cubes. Place in a small chopper bowl and blend until crumbly like breadcrumbs. You can also grate the whole block cut into cubes in a food processor. Measure out the amount required and freeze the remainder for future use.

Parmesan cheese has a strong flavour. Buy in block and grate as required. The flavour of fresh parmesan is far superior to the packaged pre-grated variety.

Lemon Coconut Cheesecake

This is an ultra light cheesecake with a tender nutty cake base. This cake makes a delightful dessert, topped with fresh fruits such as mango, kiwi or skinless orange segments.

Cake Base

Butter	**45 g, at room temperature**
Castor sugar	**25 g**
Plain (all-purpose) flour	**25 g**
Baking powder	**$^1/_2$ tsp**
Egg	**1, medium (60 g), beaten**
Ground almonds	**25 g**

Cheese Filling

Cream cheese	**125 g, at room temperature**
Castor sugar	**60 g, divided into 2 portions**
Eggs	**2 medium (60 g each), separated**
Plain (all-purpose) flour	**15 g**
Coconut cream (*pati santan*)	**75 ml**
Lemon juice	**1 Tbsp**

Topping

Chilled whipping cream	**75 ml**
Grated coconut for sprinkling	**1 Tbsp, toasted**
Flan paper cases	**5 (9 cm base by 3 cm height)**

To prepare cake base, cream butter and castor sugar in a small deep bowl until creamy, using an electric hand rotary whisk.

Sift flour and baking powder together. Beat the flour mixture and beaten egg into the butter mixture. Stir in ground almonds.

Divide into 5 equal portions and spread on bases of flan cases placed on a wire rack.

To prepare cheese filling, beat cream cheese and half of sugar (30 g) in bowl of an electric mixer until smooth and creamy.

Beat in egg yolks, one at a time. Add plain flour and mix well. Gradually beat in coconut cream until smooth. Add lemon juice.

In a separate bowl, whisk egg whites until fairly stiff. Continue beating and add remaining 30 g of castor sugar gradually.

Fold into cheese mixture, a third at a time. Spoon mixture evenly to fill prepared flan cases.

Bake in preheated oven at 160°C for 25–30 minutes until cakes are lightly golden. Turn off oven and leave cakes in the oven for about 15 minutes before removing to cool completely.

Whisk cream in a chilled bowl until soft peaks form. Fill a piping bag fitted with a star nozzle with the whipped cream and pipe a border of cream around the edges of each cake.

Sprinkle surfaces with some toasted coconut.

Makes 5 cakes

Note: Coconut cream or *pati santan*, which gives the cake a creamy flavour, is coconut milk squeezed from only the grated white of coconut without adding water.

Chocolate Cheese Cupcake

A rich luxurious cupcake topped with delicate chocolate shavings.

Ginger cookies	**30 g**
Dark chocolate	**60 g**
Cream cheese	**180 g, at room temperature**
Whipping cream	**75 ml**
Egg	**1, medium (65 g)**
Castor sugar	**20 g**
Cocoa powder	**20 g, sifted**
Topping	
Chocolate shavings	**2 Tbsp**
Icing sugar to dust	
Medium paper cases	**9 (4.5 base x 2.5 cm height)**

Line muffin pans with paper cases.

Break the ginger cookies into small pieces and place in a small hand chopper. Blend into fine breadcrumbs.

Scatter a teaspoon of ginger biscuit crumbs on each of the paper cases and set aside.

Melt the chocolate in a bowl over gently simmering water. Remove to cool.

Put cream cheese in a mixing bowl and beat for a minute. Add cream and beat until smooth. Beat in the egg, castor sugar and cocoa.

Fold in the melted chocolate and mix well. Spoon mixture evenly into the biscuit-crumb paper cases.

Bake in preheated oven at 150°C for 25–30 minutes or until cake is firm to the touch.

Turn off the oven and leave the oven door slightly ajar. Leave cake to settle for 5 minutes in the oven before removing.

Leave cakes to cool in the pan. Remove and place on a wire rack. Top with generous amounts of chocolate shavings.

Chill in the refrigerator. Just before serving, dust over with icing sugar.

Makes 9 cupcakes

Note: To make chocolate shavings, place a small block of well-chilled chocolate onto a chilled cutting board. Use a sharp knife to slice the chocolate thinly to get thin shavings. Extra shavings can be stored in a covered container in the freezer for future use.

Ginger Cheese Cupcake

Ginger adds a spicy tinge to this rich cheese cupcake.

Ginger or digestive biscuits	**55 g, broken into pieces**
Stem ginger	**15 g, optional (recipe on page 150)**
Cream cheese	**300 g, at room temperature and cut into chunks**
Castor sugar	**115 g**
Stem ginger	**20 g, chopped**
Whipping cream	**50 ml**
Lemon juice	**2 Tbsp**
Grated orange or lemon rind	**From ½ orange or lemon**
Egg	**1, large (75 g), beaten with a fork**

Topping

Chocolate shavings for decoration

Paper cases   **12 (4.5 cm base x 3.5 cm height)**

Line a 12-hole muffin pan with paper cases.

Place biscuits and ginger into a small food processor and blend into fine crumbs. Scatter a level tsp of crumble onto base of each paper case.

In bowl of a large food processor, put in cream cheese, sugar and stem ginger and blend for a few seconds.

Pour in cream, lemon juice, lemon or orange rind and beaten egg. Blend for 20 seconds just to combine ingredients, ensuring that mixture is free from lumps.

Spoon mixture evenly into prepared cases and level surface with a teaspoon.

Bake in preheated oven at 175°C for 23–25 minutes or until just set.

Leave to cool in the oven with the oven door slightly ajar for 5 minutes before removing from oven. Use a pair of sharp scissors to cut serrated edges around paper ends.

Top with chocolate shavings.

Makes 12 cupcakes

Note: The chopped stem ginger gives the cake a nice texture. Stem ginger is expensive as it requires time to prepare. You can easily make your own and they store well in a covered glass container for at least 6 months in the refrigerator.

Lychee Cheese Cupcake

A delicious and creamy cheese cupcake with a refreshing tropical flavour.

Crumb Crust Base

Digestive biscuits	**65 g**
Melted butter	**35 g**

Filling

Lychees	**230 g, drained weight from 1 can (567 g) lychees**
Gelatine	**9 g**
Lychee syrup	**2 Tbsp, from can**
Cream cheese	**125 g, at room temperature**
Castor sugar	**25 g**
Natural yoghurt	**110 ml**
Whipping cream	**125 g**

Topping

Cointreau or Draumbuie liqueur	**120 ml, or lychee syrup**
Gelatine	**$^3/_4$ tsp**
Candied orange strips for decoration	**(recipe on page 151)**
Large paper cases	**10 (5 cm base x 3.5 cm height)**

Crush biscuits in a small hand-held food processor and add melted butter. Process a few seconds until mixture is like breadcrumbs.

Line a 12-hole muffin pan with paper cases. Spread a tspful of crumb crust on each paper case and press lightly. Set aside.

Place drained lychees in a blender and blend into a fine puree. Set aside.

Sprinkle gelatine over lychee syrup and leave until spongy. Stand bowl over hot water to dissolve gelatine completely. Let it cool but not set.

Place cream cheese and castor sugar in bowl of small food processor and blend until smooth. Add yoghurt and blend until creamy.

Add lychee puree and gelatine mixture and blend again.

Whisk the cream until it begins to stiffen and fold into the cheese mixture.

Spoon mixture evenly to fill prepared paper cases up to three-quarters full. Refrigerate for at least 4 hours or overnight until firm and set.

To prepare topping, sprinkle gelatine over liqueur or lychee syrup and leave until spongy. Stand over hot water and stir well to dissolve gelatine.

Spoon topping evenly on top of cheesecakes. Leave to set in the refrigerator. Decorate with candied orange strips.

Makes 10 cupcakes

Note: In order for the cheesecakes to set properly to the right texture, make sure the gelatine is totally dissolved. Sprinkle gelatine in lychee syrup to soften in a small heatproof bowl and stand bowl in pan of hot water to come up halfway up the side. If gelatine does not dissolve, simmer gently and stir until the gelatine is dissolved and the liquid is smooth with no grainy bits.

Lemon Cream Cheese Cupcake

A light buttery cheesecake with a tart lemon icing.

Self-raising flour	**130 g**
Baking powder	**$^1/_2$ tsp**
Butter	**135 g**
Cream cheese	**100 g, at room temperature**
Castor sugar	**175 g**
Grated lemon rind	**1 tsp**
Eggs	**2, medium (60-65 g each)**
Salt	**A pinch**
Lemon juice	**1 Tbsp**
Walnuts	**30 g toasted and chopped, reserve 1 Tbsp for topping**

Lemon Glaze Icing

Icing sugar	**80 g, sifted**
Lemon juice	**1 Tbsp**

Topping

Praline pieces for decoration	**(recipe on page 150)**
Large paper cases	**12 (4.5 cm base x 3 cm height)**

Line muffin pan with paper cases.

Sift self-raising flour and baking powder together.

Cream butter and cream cheese until light and creamy. Beat in castor sugar until light and fluffy for approximately 2–3 minutes.

Beat in lemon rind and eggs, one at a time, until well combined. Fold in sifted dry ingredients, salt, lemon juice and walnuts.

Spoon mixture evenly into prepared paper cases.

Bake in preheated oven at 175°C for 15–18 minutes until light golden and a skewer inserted into the centre of the cake comes out clean.

Remove from the pan and cool on a wire rack.

Meanwhile, prepare Lemon Glaze Icing. Sift icing sugar onto a baking sheet and tip into a small mixing bowl.

Place the lemon juice in a heatproof bowl and microwave on 'high' for 15 seconds. Stir hot lemon juice into the icing sugar until smooth. Spoon into an icing bag fitted with a writing nozzle.

Pipe swirls of lemon icing on surface of each cup cake. Sprinkle some walnuts on top and decorate with praline pieces.

Makes 12 cupcakes

Chocolate Cupcakes

Chocolate Rum Raisin Cupcake

Rum and raisins lend an elegance to this recipe, giving it a rich velvety texture.

Rum	**30 ml**
Raisins	**50 g, chopped**
Butter	**85 g, diced**
Castor sugar	**75 g**
Eggs	**2, medium (60 g each), separated**
Dark chocolate	**100 g, at room temperature and melted**
Self-raising flour	**75 g, sifted**
Topping	
Vanilla ice cream	
Raspberries	**11**
Large paper cases	**11 (5.5 cm base x 3.5 cm height)**

Line muffin pan with paper cases.

Combine rum and chopped raisins in a bowl and leave to stand for at least 3 hours.

In the bowl of an electric cake mixer, cream the butter and half of the castor sugar until light and creamy. Beat in egg yolks until well combined.

Stir in rum raisin mixture, melted chocolate and the sifted flour.

In a separate bowl, whisk the egg whites until soft peaks form. Then gradually beat in the remaining half of the castor sugar until just stiff.

Fold the egg white mixture, one-third at a time, into the chocolate mixture. Spoon mixture evenly into the paper cases and level the surfaces.

Bake in preheated oven at 160°C for 20 minutes or until just firm to the touch.

Cool cake in the pan. Just before serving, place a small scoop of vanilla ice cream and raspberry on the cake.

Makes 11 cupcakes

Note: To melt the chocolate, place in a bowl and microwave for 30 seconds on high. This cupcake improves with keeping. Store in an airtight container in the freezer for 1–2 weeks. Warm through before serving.

Nutella Chocolate Hazelnut Cupcake

This nutty flavoured chocolate cake are flourless and has a fudge-like texture. Use good quality chocolate for a soft smooth texture.

Dark chocolate	100 g, chopped
Butter	65 g, at room temperature
Nutella (chocolate hazelnut spread)	100 g
Eggs	2, large (75 g each), separated
Brown sugar	75 g
Ground almonds	100 g
Topping	
Fresh whipped cream (optional)	
Fresh raspberries	10
Fresh mint leaves	10, small
Large paper cases	10 (4.5 cm base x 3.5 cm height)

Line a muffin pan with the paper cases.

Place chocolate, butter and Nutella in a bowl over a saucepan of gently simmering water. Stir until melted and smooth. Remove and set aside to cool.

Whisk egg yolks and sugar until pale, thick and light. Stir in almonds and the chocolate mixture.

Whisk egg whites until firm peaks form. Fold, one-third at a time, into the chocolate mixture.

Spoon mixture evenly to fill prepared paper cases and level surfaces with a teaspoon.

Bake in preheated oven at 175°C for 25 minutes or until a skewer inserted into the centre of the cake comes out clean.

Cool cakes in pan. Remove cakes when cook and if desired, top with fresh cream, a raspberry and a mint leaf on each cake.

Makes 10 cupcakes

Chocolate Walnut Cupcake with Chocolate Icing

Serve this delicious crunchy cupcake slightly warm to enjoy its true goodness.

Good quality dark chocolate	**85 g, at room temperature and chopped**
Self-raising flour	**75 g**
Bicarbonate of soda	**$1/4$ tsp**
Butter	**65 g, at room temperature**
Castor sugar	**75 g, divided into 2 portions**
Eggs	**3, medium (60 g each), separated**
Milk	**1 Tbsp, at room temperature**
Chocolate Icing	
Good quality dark chocolate	**80 g, chopped**
Reduced or single cream	**75 ml**
Topping	
Whole walnuts	**12, toasted**
Large paper cases	**12 (5 cm base x 3.5 cm height)**

Line a muffin pan with the paper cases.

Melt chocolate in a saucepan over gently simmering water. Set aside to cool.

Sift the self-raising flour and bicarbonate of soda together.

In a mixing bowl, cream butter with half of the sugar until light and creamy.

Beat in egg yolks, one at a time, followed by the cooled melted chocolate and milk. Fold in sifted ingredients.

In a separate bowl, whisk the egg whites until soft peaks form. Then beat in remaining sugar, half at a time, until mixture is just stiff.

Spoon mixture evenly into prepared cases.

Bake in preheated oven at 160°C for 25 minutes or until a skewer inserted into the centre of the cake comes out clean.

Cool cakes in the pan then remove.

Meanwhile, prepare icing by melting chocolate in a saucepan over simmering water and stir in cream until smooth. Cool slightly.

Cover cupcakes with chocolate icing. Top each cake with a walnut.

Makes 12 cupcakes

Note: Reduced cream is a pure dairy sterilised cream with 25% milk fat. It comes in 170 g cans.

Moist Chocolate Cupcake

This chocolate cupcake has a rich chocolatey flavour if you use good quality chocolate with 70% cocoa solids.

Dark chocolate	**85 g**
Butter	**75 g**
Icing sugar	**75 g, sifted**
Eggs	**2, large (70–75 g each), separated**
Vanilla essence	**1 tsp**
Self-raising flour	**40 g, sifted**
Ground almonds	**30 g**

Topping

Icing sugar or cocoa powder to dust	
Large paper cases	**10 (4.5 cm base x 3.5 cm height)**

Line a muffin pan with the paper cases.

Place chocolate in a heatproof bowl over gently simmering water and stir until chocolate melts. Remove and set aside.

Place butter and sugar in a mixing bowl and beat until light and fluffy. Beat in egg yolks, one at a time, beating well after each addition.

Add vanilla essence. Stir in flour and ground almonds.

Whisk egg whites in a separate bowl until just stiff. Fold into the main mixture, half at a time.

Spoon mixture evenly to fill prepared paper cases.

Bake in preheated oven at 190°C for 15–18 minutes or until a skewer inserted into the centre of the cake comes out clean.

Cool cakes in the pan. Remove and dust with icing sugar or cocoa powder.

Makes 10 cupcakes

Truffle Cupcake Delight

This exotic truffle cupcake is a classy one to serve for dessert. With its rich dark chocolate cream, this is definitely a winner when you have friends over for dinner.

Cocoa powder	**20 g**
Corn flour (cornstarch)	**12 g**
Eggs	**3, large (70 g each), separated**
Icing sugar	**65 g, sifted**

Rich Chocolate Cream

Dark chocolate	**100 g, chopped**
Thickened cream	**120 ml**

Topping

Grated white chocolate, chilled for sprinkling	
White chocolate decorations	
Medium paper cases	**12 (4.5 cm base x 2.5 cm height)**

Grease sides and line bases of a 12-hole muffin pan with non-stick paper.

Sift cocoa powder and corn flour together.

Whisk egg yolks and icing sugar until pale and thick. Carefully fold in sifted ingredients, half at a time.

Whisk the egg whites in a separate bowl with a hand-held electric whisk until soft peaks form. Gently fold into cocoa mixture, half at a time.

Spoon mixture evenly into prepared pan.

Bake in preheated oven at 175°C for 15 minutes or until cooked through when tested with a wooden skewer.

Cool cakes in the pan. Cakes will leave the sides of the pan when cool. Turn out onto a wire rack to cool completely. Remove base lining paper.

Melt chocolate and cream in a heatproof bowl over gently simmering water. Stir to mix well.

Spread chocolate cream to cover the surface and sprinkle 1 tsp of grated white chocolate on top. Decorate with a piece of white chocolate decoration.

Place cakes into the paper cases. Refrigerate and serve chilled.

Makes 12 cupcakes

Note: Cream is the fat separated from milk. Thickened cream contains 35% fat. It is thickened with gelatine or vegetable gum. It is wonderful for whipping as it holds its shape. If not available, replace with whipping cream with 35% fat. Ensure that the cream is well chilled before beating.

Use good quality cocoa to enjoy the flavours of this chocolate cake. Good cocoa powder should have a minimum cocoa butter content of 20% and the cocoa should be a dark mahogany brown.

Mud Cupcake

A rich fudge-like chocolate cake containing no flour.

Cocoa powder	20 g, sifted
Boiling hot water	65 ml
Dark chocolate	75 g, melted
Butter	75 g, at room temperature, melted
Brown sugar	120 g
Ground almonds	65 g
Eggs	2, large (70–75 g each), separated
Topping	
Sugar dredgees for sprinkling	
Paper cases	9 (5.5 cm base x 3.5 cm height)

Line muffin pan with paper cases.

Combine cocoa powder and hot water in a mixing bowl and stir until smooth. Add chocolate, butter, sugar and ground almonds and mix well.

Beat in egg yolks, one at a time, using a hand-held electric whisk.

In a separate bowl, whisk the egg whites until soft peaks form. Fold into the chocolate mixture in three batches.

Fill paper cups with batter up to three-quarter full.

Bake in preheated oven at 175°C for 30 minutes or until firm. Cool in the pan.

Remove cakes and sprinkle with colourful dredgees.

Makes 9 cupcakes

Note: Take care that the egg whites are not beaten until too stiff. Beaten until soft peaks form means the beaten whites will still look and feel moist, and hold their shape in sharp peaks that droop just slightly after the beater is lifted. If the egg whites are over-beaten, they will look dry and the whole mass will break apart into chunks. When they are this stiff, it is difficult to fold into the other ingredients without deflating the air bubbles.

Chocolate Mixed Fruit Walnut Cupcake

A no-flour chocolate flavoured cake with mixed fruits, all nice and moist from soaking in brandy or orange juice.

Mixed fruits	60 g, chopped
Brandy or orange juice	65 ml
Ground walnuts	60 g
Fresh white breadcrumbs	15 g
Butter	65 g
Castor sugar	50 g
Egg	1, large (75 g)
Plain dark chocolate	65 g, melted
Topping	
Red cherry	1, cut into 9 pieces
Some rice crispies	
Large paper cases	9 (4.5 cm base x 3.5 cm height)

Line muffin pan with paper cases.

Place mixed fruits and brandy or orange juice in a small saucepan and bring to a boil. Boil, uncovered, until about a tablespoon of liquid remains. Transfer to a bowl to cool.

Combine ground walnuts and breadcrumbs.

Cream butter and sugar until light and fluffy. Beat in the egg for about 1 minute. Stir in walnut mixture, mixed fruits and melted chocolate.

Spoon mixture evenly to fill paper cases. Level surfaces with a teaspoon.

Bake in preheated oven at 175°C for 25 minutes or until cooked through when tested with a wooden skewer.

Cool cakes in the pan for 10 minutes before transferring onto a wire rack to cool completely.

Place a piece of cherry on centre of each cake and surround with rice crispies to form a daisy.

Makes 9 cupcakes

Photo on page 38–39

Hazelnut and Almond Chocolate Cupcake

This is an indulgent chocolate cake full of nuts.

Butter	**115 g, diced**
Light brown sugar	**110 g**
Dark chocolate	**115 g, melted and cooled**
Vanilla essence	**1 tsp**
Eggs	**3, large (70–75 g each)**
Finely ground almonds	**75 g**
Finely ground hazelnuts	**40 g**

Topping
Fresh cream
Small white chocolate triangles
Fresh cranberries

Large paper cases	**12 (5 cm base x 3.5 cm height)**

Line a 12-hole muffin pan with the paper cases.

In bowl of electric cake mixer, cream butter with castor sugar until light and fluffy. Beat in cooled melted chocolate and vanilla essence.

Combine ground almonds and hazelnuts together.

Beat in eggs, one at a time, beating well after each addition. Lastly fold in ground almonds and hazelnuts.

Spoon mixture evenly to fill prepared paper cases.

Bake in preheated oven at 175°C for 30 minutes or until a skewer inserted into the centre of the cake comes out clean.

Cool cakes in the pan. Top with fresh cream, white chocolate triangles and cranberries.

Makes 12 cupcakes

Note: Ensure the almonds and hazelnuts are finely ground. This can easily be done by placing nuts in a coffee grinder and then grinding in spurts to prevent lumps from forming.

Brandy Chocolate Cupcake with Chocolate Mirror Icing

Brandy gives this cupcake a rich taste and is even more attractive with chocolate mirror icing.

Self-raising flour	**110 g**
Cocoa powder	**12 g**
Butter	**125 g, diced**
Castor sugar	**120 g**
Eggs	**3, medium (60 g each)**
Milk	**1 Tbsp, combined with 1$^1/_2$ Tbsp brandy or fresh orange juice**
Almond flakes	**25 g crushed**
Brandy	**1 Tbsp, combined with 2 Tbsp fresh orange juice, for drizzling**

Chocolate Mirror Icing

Castor sugar	**60 g**
Cocoa	**20 g, sifted**
Liquid glucose	**85 g**
Water	**2 Tbsp**
Dark chocolate	**50 g, chopped**
Butter	**50 g, at room temperature**
Vanilla essence	**$^1/_2$ tsp**
Salt	**A pinch**

Topping

Pink and white soft sweets, trimmed to form flower centre and petals	
Large paper cases	**12 (5 cm base x 3.5 cm height)**

Line a 12-hole muffin pan with the paper cases.

Sift the self-raising flour and cocoa powder together.

In bowl of electric mixer, cream butter with castor sugar until light and creamy. Gradually beat in the eggs, one at a time.

Fold in sifted ingredients alternating with the combined milk/brandy mixture. Stir in almond flakes.

Spoon mixture evenly to fill prepared paper cases.

Bake in preheated oven at 175°C for 20 minutes or until a skewer inserted into the centre of a cake comes out clean.

Remove from oven. Drizzle over brandy/orange mixture. Stand in the pan to cool.

Spread a tspful of chocolate mirror icing on each cake. It is easier to spread icing when cakes are still warm. So prepare icing while cakes are still in the oven.

Place a piece of pink soft sweet on the centre and 6 white soft sweet petals to form a flower on cupcakes.

* To Make Chocolate Mirror Icing

Place sugar, cocoa, glucose and water in a non-stick saucepan over low heat. Bring slowly to the boil, stirring constantly. Simmer for 1 minute.

Remove from heat, add the chopped chocolate and stir until smooth. Beat in the butter, essence and salt and continue to beat until completely smooth and icing begins to thicken.

Use immediately.

Makes 12 cupcakes

Note: Brandy can be substituted with fresh orange juice.

Tiramisu Cupcake

This rich tiramisu cake is a must-have when entertaining guests at home.

Self-raising flour	45 g
Good quality cocoa powder	15 g
Eggs	2, large (70–75 g each)
Castor sugar	60 g
Sunflower or corn oil	1¹/₂ Tbsp
Coffee Rum Syrup	
Granulated sugar	60 g
Instant coffee granules	1 Tbsp
Boiling hot water	100 ml
Rum	1¹/₂ Tbsp, or 1 tsp vanilla essence
Cream Cheese Icing	
Cream cheese	125 g, diced
Rum	1 Tbsp, or 1 tsp vanilla essence
Whipping or double cream	75 ml
Topping	
Cocoa powder for dusting	1–2 tsp
Medium paper cases	10

Grease sides and line bases of 10 muffin pans with non-stick paper.

Sift self-raising flour and cocoa powder together.

In bowl of electric cake mixer fitted with a balloon whisk, beat eggs and sugar until really thick and creamy. Gently fold in sifted ingredients followed by sunflower or corn oil, taking care not to deflate the mixture.

Spoon mixture evenly into prepared pans.

Bake in preheated oven at 175°C for 25 minutes or until springy to the touch. Leave to cool in the pan and run a small butter knife around the edges to loosen cakes.

Leave cakes in the pan and prick each cake all over with a wooden skewer. Drizzle warm coffee rum syrup equally over the cakes, 1 tablespoon at a time. Allow syrup to soak before drizzling more. After drizzling, let cakes soak for at least 2 hours.

Turn cakes out carefully, remove lining paper and place on paper cases. Spread or pipe a large rosette of cream cheese icing on top.

Dust with cocoa powder. Chill thoroughly before serving.

* To Prepare Coffee Rum Syrup

Put sugar and coffee in a measuring jug. Pour in boiling water and stir well to dissolve. Stir in rum or vanilla essence and top with water to make 150 ml.

* To Make Cream Cheese Icing

Place cheese in a small food chopper or processor and pulse until smooth and free from lumps. Beat in rum or vanilla essence.

In a chilled bowl, beat cream until soft peaks form. Add to cheese mixture and mix together until combined. Use immediately.

Makes 10 cupcakes

Triple Chocolate Apple Cupcake

An awesome combination of dark and white chocolate with green apples.

Plain (all-purpose) flour	75 g
Bicarbonate of soda	$^1/_4$ tsp
Baking powder	$^1/_4$ tsp
Green apples	75 g, peeled and cut into chunks
Dark plain chocolate	90 g, chopped
Castor sugar	105 g
Soft margarine	30 g
Egg whites	2, large, lightly beaten
Salt	A pinch
Vanilla essence	$^1/_2$ tsp
Pecan or walnuts	60 g, chopped
Chocolate chips	50 g
White chocolate buttons	50 g, chopped
Medium paper cups	12 (4 cm base x 2 cm height)

Sift the flour, bicarbonate of soda and baking powder together.

Puree the apples in a small chopper bowl and pour into a small heatproof saucepan.

Put in the plain chocolate, sugar and margarine. Stir over low heat until chocolate melts and mixture is smooth. Remove from heat and cool.

Pour into bowl of electric mixer. Add egg whites and beat for 1 minute.

Stir in sifted ingredients, salt and vanilla essence. Mix in nuts, chocolate chips and white chocolate.

Fill paper cups with chocolate batter, dividing evenly.

Bake in preheated oven at 175°C for 25 minutes or until just set.

Makes 12 cupcakes

Chocolate Banana Brownie Cupcake

This is a fabulous brownie, rich and decadent with bananas.

Butter	**90 g, at room temperature**
Plain chocolate	**80 g, at room temperature and chopped**
Eggs	**2, large (70–75 g each)**
Vanilla essence	**$^1/_2$ tsp**
Salt	**$^1/_4$ tsp**
Light brown sugar	**155 g**
Self-raising flour	**90 g, sifted**
Pecans	**60 g, coarsely chopped,**
Ripe bananas	**100 g, peeled and diced**
Dark or button chocolate	**60 g, chopped and frozen**
Large paper cases	**12 (5 cm base x 3.5 cm height)**

Line muffin pan with paper cases.

In a heatproof bowl over gently simmering water, melt butter and chocolate together stirring well until combined. Set aside to cool.

Place eggs, vanilla essence, salt and sugar in a medium mixing bowl and whisk with a hand-held electric whisk until well combined.

Use the electric beater on low speed to fold in the flour followed by the melted chocolate mixture. Stir in pecans, bananas and chopped cold chocolate.

Spoon mixture evenly into paper cases up to two-thirds full.

Bake in preheated oven at 175°C for 30 minutes or until cooked through when tested with a wooden skewer.

Makes 12 cupcakes

Note: If desired, sprinkle some crushed banana chips over cupcakes.

Chocolate Coffee Cupcake

This cake is a heavenly treat. Use good quality chocolate. It keeps and stores well in a covered container for several days in the refrigerator.

Dark chocolate	**125 g**
Instant coffee powder	**1 heaped tsp**
Hot water	**1 Tbsp**
Cold butter	**125 g, diced**
Castor sugar	**120 g**
Eggs	**3, large (70–75 g each), separated**
Vanilla essence	**$^1/_2$ tsp**
Ground almonds	**50 g**
Salt	**A pinch**
Plain (all-purpose) flour	**50 g, sifted**

Chocolate Coffee Icing

Dark chocolate	**65 g**
Instant coffee powder	**1 tsp**
Whipping cream	**40 ml**

Topping

White chocolate shavings for decoration

Large paper cases	**12 (4.5 cm base x 3.5 cm height)**

Line a 12-hole muffin pan with the paper cases.

Melt chocolate in a heatproof bowl over a pan of gently simmering water. Remove and cool.

Dissolve coffee powder in hot water and set aside.

Cream butter and sugar until pale and light. Beat in egg yolks, one at a time, and the vanilla essence.

Stir in chocolate and coffee mixture. Fold in ground almonds.

In a separate bowl, whisk the egg whites with salt using a hand-held electric beater until just stiff.

Gradually fold into main mixture, alternating with the plain flour.

Spoon mixture evenly to fill prepared paper cases.

Bake in preheated oven at 175°C for 25 minutes or until a skewer inserted into the centre of a cake comes out clean.

Cool cakes in the pan.

Meanwhile, prepare chocolate coffee icing. Place chocolate in a heatproof bowl over simmering water. Stir occasionally until smooth.

Add coffee powder and cream and beat until smooth.

Remove cakes from pan. Pipe chocolate coffee icing on cakes. Decorate with white chocolate shavings.

Makes 12 cupcakes

Note: White chocolate does not contain cocoa solids and is really not chocolate at all. It is made from cocoa butter, sugar, milk and vanilla. Avoid buying white chocolate that contains vegetable oils instead of cocoa butter.

Sour Cream Chocolate Cupcake with Chocolate Glaze Icing

This is a tender moist chocolate cake with a rich chocolate icing. The chocolate icing will spread more easily when the cake is still warm.

Self-raising flour	90 g
Cocoa powder	30 g
Bicarbonate of soda	$^1/_4$ tsp
Butter	90 g
Soft brown sugar	120 g
Egg	1, large (70 g)
Sour cream or yoghurt	75 ml, combined with 2 Tbsp milk

Chocolate Glaze Icing

Plain chocolate	35 g
Milk	1 Tbsp
Butter	15 g
Icing sugar	45 g, sifted
Cocoa powder	8 g, sifted
Large paper cases	10 (4.5 cm base x 3.5 cm height)

Line a muffin pan with the paper cases.

Sift self-raising flour, cocoa powder and bicarbonate of soda together.

Cream butter and sugar until light and fluffy. Beat in the egg for 1 minute.

Beat in sour cream mixture, half at a time. Fold in sifted ingredients.

Spoon mixture evenly to fill prepared paper cases. Level surfaces with a teaspoon

Bake in preheated oven at 175° for 15–18 minutes or until a skewer inserted into the centre of the cake comes out clean.

Cool cakes in the pan.

Meanwhile, prepare chocolate icing by placing chocolate, milk and butter in a bowl over simmering water. Stir until melted and combined. Add sifted ingredients. Beat well with a spoon until icing is thick and smooth.

Remove cupcakes and spoon icing onto cupcakes, smoothening the tops to cover the cakes.

Makes 10 cupcakes

Walnut and Double Chocolate Cupcake

This is a wonderful light cupcake using only egg whites and full of nuts and chocolate. You can use pistachios or hazelnuts instead of walnuts.

Walnuts	**125 g, toasted and coarsely chopped**
Dark chocolate	**120 g, coarsely chopped**
Cocoa powder	**$^1/_2$ Tbsp (4 g), sifted**
Eggs	**4, medium (60 g each), separated for whites only**
Castor sugar	**70 g**
Plain (all-purpose) flour	**25 g, sifted**

Topping (optional)
Whipped cream

Sliced strawberries or whole raspberries

Large paper cases	**15 (4.5 cm base x 3.5 cm height)**

Line muffin pans with the paper cases.

In bowl of an electric cake mixer, combine walnuts, chocolate and cocoa powder and mix well. Set aside.

In bowl of an electric cake mixer, beat egg whites with a balloon whisk until soft peaks form. Add sugar, a tablespoon at a time, and continue beating until mixture forms stiff peaks but is still glossy.

On lowest speed of mixer, mix in one-third of the walnut mixture. Gently fold in remaining mixture and flour with a large metal spoon until combined.

Spoon mixture evenly to fill prepared paper cases.

Bake in preheated oven at 175°C for 25 minutes or until a skewer inserted into the centre of a cake comes out clean.

Cool cakes in the pan.

If desired, serve with whipped cream topped with strawberries or raspberries.

Makes 15 cupcakes

Chocolate Almond Cupcake with Chocolate Icing

A decadent almond cupcake with a delightful chocolate icing for a special weekend tea.

Dark plain chocolate	**50 g, chopped**
Butter	**65 g, at room temperature**
Castor sugar	**50 g**
Eggs	**2, large (70 g each), separated**
Ground almonds	**50 g**
Fresh brown breadcrumbs	**25 g**
Apricot jam	**15 g, combined with ¹/₂ Tbsp boiling water**

Chocolate Icing

Dark plain chocolate	**100 g, chopped**
Butter	**30 g, at room temperature**
Milk	**¹/₂ Tbsp**

Topping

Spiral soft sweets	**9**
Large paper cases	**9 (4.5 cm base x 3.5 cm height)**

Line muffin pan with paper cases.

In a heatproof bowl over gently simmering water, melt chocolate and set aside.

Cream butter and sugar in a mixing bowl using a hand-held whisk until light and fluffy. Beat in the egg yolks all at once.

Beat in almonds and breadcrumbs and then the chocolate until just combined.

In a separate bowl, whisk the egg whites until just stiff. Fold into the main mixture in three batches.

Spoon mixture evenly into paper cases and level surfaces with the back of a teaspoon.

Bake in preheated oven at 175°C for 20 minutes or until cooked through when tested with a wooden skewer.

Cool cakes in the pan. Brush the tops with melted apricot jam mixture.

Meanwhile, prepare chocolate icing by placing chocolate and butter in a heatproof bowl over simmering water. Stir into a smooth mixture. Remove from heat.

Remove cakes from pan. Pipe chocolate icing on top of cakes. Arrange spiral soft sweets on centres of cakes.

Makes 9 cupcakes

Note: Soft sweets can be found at candy counters in supermarkets.

Cream and Jam Cupcakes

Peach and Passionfruit Streusel Cupcake

A delicious moist cake with a soft centre of fruit and jam and topped with a nutty crunchy crumble. Makes an attractive dessert when entertaining.

Plain (all-purpose) flour	175 g, sifted	
Cold butter	90 g, diced	
Castor sugar	60 g	
Baking powder	$^1/_2$ tsp	
Egg	1, large (70 g), combined with 1 tsp vanilla essence and whisked until frothy	
Raspberry or strawberry jam	2 Tbsp	
Passionfruit pulp	60 g	
Peach halves	2, cut into thin slices	
Almond flakes	25 g	
Castor sugar	½ Tbsp	
Large paper cases	9 (4.5 cm base x 3.5 cm height)	

Line muffin pan with paper cases.

Place sifted flour and cold butter into bowl of a food processor fitted with a cutting blade. Blend until crumbly. Stir in castor sugar and pulse to mix well.

Measure out 100 g of the fine crumbs into a bowl and set aside for topping.

Add baking powder, beaten egg mixture and passionfruit pulp to the remaining mixture in the food processor and process again.

Spoon mixture evenly to fill paper cases. Level surfaces with a teaspoon.

Place half a teaspoonful of jam on the centre of each cake. Arrange 2 slices of peach on top.

Mix almond flakes with the 100 g of reserved crumbs and sprinkle over jam and peaches. Sprinkle some castor sugar over the almond crumb mixture.

Bake in preheated oven at 175°C (fan oven) for 25 minutes or until light golden in colour. Cool cakes in the pan. Remove and serve.

Makes 9 cupcakes

Timeless Butterfly Cupcake

A timeless classic for children's parties and even for those who are still kids at heart.

Butter	60 g
Castor sugar	60 g
Egg	1, medium (65 g), beaten with a fork
Vanilla essence	1/4 tsp
Self-raising flour	60 g, sifted
Low-fat milk	2 Tbsp
Strawberry jam or any jam of your choice	60 g
Whipping or thickened cream	120 ml
Decoration	
Red coloured sugar dredgees for decoration	16
Icing sugar for dusting	
Medium paper cases	8 (4 cm base by 2.5 cm height)

Line patty tins with paper cases.

Place butter and sugar in a deep mixing bowl and beat together with an electric hand-held whisk until light and creamy. Gradually beat in the egg and essence.

Fold in flour and sufficient milk to make a soft dropping consistency.

Spoon mixture evenly into prepared cases and level surfaces with a teaspoon.

Bake in preheated oven at 175°C for 15 minutes or until cooked through when tested with a wooden skewer.

Cool in the tins for 10 minutes, then transfer onto a wire rack to cool completely.

Cut a 1-cm thick circle from the top of the cakes Spread ½ tspful of jam into the cavities.

Fit a piping bag with a star nozzle and fill with cream. Pipe circles of cream to cover jam.

Cut each circle of cake in half and arrange them as a pair of wings on top of the cream. Pipe a length of cream between the wings.

Place sugar dredgees to represent eyes. If desired, dust with some icing sugar.

Makes 8 cupcakes

Photo on page 58-59

Buttery Jam and Cream Cupcake

A light and buttery cupcake served with cream and jam.

Butter	90 g, at room temperature
Eggs	2, large (70–75 g each)
Castor sugar	90 g
Vanilla essence	$^1/_2$ tsp
Self-raising flour	90 g, sifted
Hot water	2 Tbsp
Topping	
Strawberry Spreadable 100% Fruit Jam	
Thickened cream	150 ml, whipped
Large paper cases	12 (5.5 cm base x 3.5 cm height)

Line a 12-hole muffin pan with paper cases.

Melt butter in a microwave oven on high for 30 seconds. Set aside.

Whisk eggs in bowl of an electric cake mixer for 1 minute. Add sugar and vanilla essence and continue to whisk until pale, light and thick. The mixture should hold a trail of the whisk for 5–10 seconds.

Carefully fold in the melted butter and flour, one-third at a time. The butter should be poured in a stream around the edge of the bowl and then folded in. If the butter is poured heavily on top of the mixture, it will deflate air in the mixture.

Fold in hot water and mix well.

Spoon mixture evenly into prepared cases up to two-thirds full and level surfaces with the back of a teaspoon.

Bake in preheated oven at 175°C for 23–25 minutes or until well risen and cooked through when tested with a wooden skewer.

Cool cakes in pan. Remove and place on a wire rack.

Spread a teaspoonful of jam on top. Whip the cream until firm peaks form. Fill a piping bag fitted with a star nozzle with the whipped cream and pipe a large rosette over the jam.

Makes 12 cupcakes

Note: Never use too hot an oven for this recipe as you can easily over-brown the surfaces. If this happens the cakes are inclined to sink badly in the centres because the heat does not evenly penetrate through the surface crust. Bake the tray of cakes on the centre shelf of the oven.

Use a good quality 100% fruit jam as it is less sweet and imparts a wonderful fruity flavour to these airy buttery sponge cakes. An example of a brand of this jam is IXL. The jam is made only from fruit and sweetened with fruit juices with no cane sugar added.

Surprise Cupcake

Kids will love this simple-to-make cupcake with its colourful decorations.

Self-raising flour	130 g
Baking powder	1 tsp
Butter	85 g, at room temperature
Sugar	40 g
Egg	1, medium (65 g)
Vanilla essence	$^1/_2$ tsp
Salt	A pinch
Low-fat milk	75 ml
Topping	
Fruit of the Forest or any mixed fruit jam	2 Tbsp
Thickened or whipping cream	100 ml
Kiwi fruit and strawberry slices for decoration	
Large paper cases	8 (5 cm base x 3.5 cm height)

Sift the self-raising flour and baking powder together.

Place butter and sugar in a deep mixing bowl and beat until well combined using a hand-held rotary whisk. Beat in egg and vanilla essence until light and fluffy.

Fold in sifted ingredients and salt. Lastly stir in milk.

Spoon half of the mixture to fill paper cases and level surfaces with the back of a teaspoon. Place ½ tspful of jam in each cupcake. Cover jam with remaining mixture.

Bake in preheated oven at 175°C for 18–20 minutes until firm to the touch and cooked through when tested with a wooden skewer.

Cool cakes in pan for 10 minutes. Remove and place on a wire rack to cool completely.

Whip the cream until firm peaks form and pipe decoratively on the surfaces of the cakes. Top with kiwi fruit and strawberry slices.

Makes 8 cupcakes

Note: For smaller amounts of the cake mixture, you will get better, lighter and more airy results by using an electric hand-held beater or whisk than a large free-standing mixer.

Fruit Cupcakes

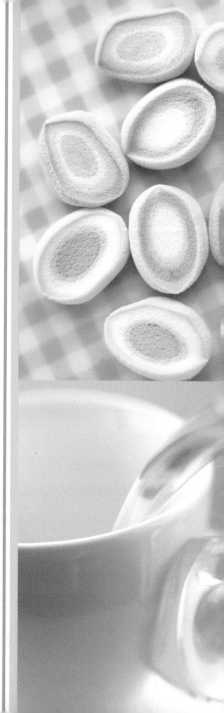

Banana Apricot and Raisin Cupcake

This is incredibly easy to make and fun to eat.

Butter	**75 g**
Brown sugar	**85 g**
Eggs	**2, medium (60 g each), beaten with a fork**
Self-raising flour	**110 g**
Bicarbonate of soda	**$^1/_8$ tsp**
Ripe bananas	**150 g, peeled and mashed**
Dried apricots	**45 g, chopped**
Raisins	**30 g, chopped**
Milk	**2 Tbsp**
Topping	
Apricot jam	**1 Tbsp**
Water	**$^1/_2$ Tbsp**
Nestum cereal	**3 heaped Tbsp**
Medium paper cases	**12 (4 cm base x 2.5 cm height**

Line patty tins with paper cases.

Cream the butter and sugar until pale and fluffy in bowl of electric cake mixer. Gradually beat in the eggs, one at a time.

Sift self-raising flour and bicarbonate of soda together.

Add mashed bananas, apricots and raisins. Turn on mixer for 1 minute, put in sifted ingredients and beat for a further minute. Stir in milk.

Spoon mixture evenly into prepared patty tins.

Bake in preheated oven at 175°C for 20 minutes or until cooked through when tested with a wooden skewer.

Turn cakes out onto a wire rack.

Place apricot jam and water in a bowl and microwave on high for 30 seconds.

Brush surfaces of cakes with heated apricot jam mixture. Dip cakes into bowl of Nestum cereal to coat completely.

Place cakes in decorative paper cases.

Makes 12 cupcakes

Note: It is essential to use ripe bananas when making banana cake; if not the result will taste 'raw and sappy' and the cake will be less moist. It is even better to use over-ripe bananas than green bananas. Good bananas to use are *pisang rastali*, *pisang embun* and *pisang berangan*.

Sticky Date Cupcake with Caramel Syrup or Rich Caramel Sauce

This is a perfectly scrumptious holiday snack.

Dates	**125 g, pitted and chopped coarsely**
Water	**200 ml**
Vanilla essence	**1 tsp**
Bicarbonate of soda	**6 g (1 tsp)**
Butter	**45 g, at room temperature**
Brown sugar	**45 g**
Eggs	**2, medium (60 g each)**
Self-raising flour	**100 g, sifted**
Caramel Syrup	
Coarse sugar	**55 g**
Water	**80 ml**
Boiling water	**45 ml, or half brandy and half water mixture**
Rich Caramel Sauce	
Butter	**65 g, at room temperature**
Whipping cream	**30 ml**
Brown or light muscovado sugar	**45 g**
Vanilla essence	**¹/₂ tsp**
Brandy or orange juice	**1 Tbsp**
Large paper cases	**10 (5 cm base x 3.5 cm height)**

Line muffin pan with paper cases.

Place dates and water in a small saucepan and bring to the boil, stirring occasionally. Stir in vanilla essence and simmer, uncovered, over medium heat for 1–2 minutes.

Remove from heat and stir in bicarbonate of soda, which will foam in the saucepan and subside. Set aside to cool.

Meanwhile, cream butter and sugar using an electric mixer. Beat in eggs, one at a time, beating each egg for 15 seconds just to combine with the butter mixture.

Fold in flour evenly. Stir in lukewarm date mixture.

Spoon mixture evenly to fill paper cases. Level surfaces with a teaspoon.

Bake in preheated oven at 175°C for 23–25 minutes or until cooked through when tested with a wooden skewer.

If using Caramel Syrup, use a wooden skewer to prick surfaces of the cakes and drizzle about 1–2 tsp of caramel syrup onto the cakes. Let the syrup seep through.

If using Rich Caramel Sauce, spoon sauce over warm cupcakes to cover cakes. If desired, serve with whipped cream. Top with a small strawberry wedge.

* To Prepare Caramel Syrup

Place sugar and water in a small saucepan and bring to the boil, without stirring until liquid turns a dark golden brown. Stir in hot water or brandy/water mixture until caramel is diluted into a syrupy liquid.

* To Prepare Rich Caramel Sauce

Place all ingredients in a small saucepan and bring to a gentle boil, stirring until caramel is smooth. Simmer for 1 minute.

Makes 10 cupcakes

Apple Cider Cupcake

This light cupcake has a hidden treasure in the apple cubes.

Butter	25 g
Granulated sugar	50 g
Green apples	2, small (125 g each), peeled, cored and diced into 0.5-cm cubes
Self-raising flour	175 g
Baking powder	$^1/_2$ tsp
Mixed spice	1 tsp
Butter	120 g, at room temperature
Brown sugar	110 g
Grated lemon rind	From 1 lemon
Eggs	2, large (70 g each)
Cider vinegar	3 Tbsp
Sultanas	50 g
Topping	
Grated fresh white coconut	
Large paper cases	12 (5 cm base x 3.5 cm height)

Line muffin pan with paper cases.

Heat butter and sugar in a non-stick saucepan. Stir until butter melts and sugar begins to brown. Add apples and stir until combined. Set aside to cool.

Sift self-raising flour, baking powder and mixed spice together.

In bowl of an electric mixer, cream butter, sugar and lemon rind until light and fluffy. Beat in eggs, one at a time.

Fold in dry ingredients alternately with cider vinegar. Stir in apple butter mixture, one-third at a time. Fold in sultanas.

Spoon mixture evenly to fill paper cases. Level surfaces with a teaspoon. Sprinkle over some grated coconut.

Bake in preheated oven at 175°C for 20–23 minutes or until cooked through when tested with a wooden skewer.

Makes 12 cupcakes

Note: Do not over-brown sugar with the melted butter or the caramel will harden into lumps when apples are added.

Mango Sour Cream Cupcake

This mango cupcake has an added tangy flavour with the use of sour cream.

Self-raising flour	100 g
Bicarbonate of soda	$^1/_4$ tsp
Fragrant mango flesh	120 g
Sour cream	30 g
Grated lemon rind	1 tsp
Vanilla essence	$^1/_2$ tsp
Butter	75 g
Castor sugar	70 g
Egg	1, large (70 g)

Topping

Mango flesh	80 g, diced into 1-cm cubes
Large paper cases	9 (4.5 cm base x 3.5 cm height)

Line muffin pan with paper cases.

Sift self-raising flour and bicarbonate of soda together.

Blend mango, sour cream, lemon rind and vanilla essence in an electric blender or chopper. Set aside.

Cream butter and castor sugar in a mixing bowl with a hand-held mixer until pale and fluffy. Beat in the egg for 1 minute.

Fold in sifted ingredients alternating with the pureed mango.

Spoon mixture evenly into cases and level surfaces with a teaspoon. Place 3 cubes of mango on surface of each cupcake.

Bake in preheated oven at 175°C for 20–25 minutes until well risen and cake is cooked through when tested with a wooden skewer.

Remove from oven and cool in the pan for 10 minutes before placing on wire rack to cool completely.

Makes 9 cupcakes

Note: Choose ripe mangoes such as *Harum Manis* or Indian mangoes for their fragrance and colour. Bananas are an equally good alternative for this recipe. For the cubes of mango or banana used for topping, stir in a teaspoon of lime juice to prevent them discolouring if you are keeping the cupcakes for 1–2 days.

Jackfruit Cupcake

A delicious teatime treat. Choose fragrant ripe jackfruit. Cake stores well in an airtight container in the refrigerator. To serve, microwave on high for 30 seconds.

Butter	125 g, diced
Plain (all-purpose) flour	125 g
Baking powder	$^1/_2$ tsp
Bicarbonate of soda	A pinch
Castor sugar	50 g
Egg	1, large (70–75 g)
Condensed milk	180 ml
Honey jackfruit	125 g, seeded and coarsely chopped
Topping	
Fresh jackfruit slices for decoration	
Large paper cases	10 (5.5 cm base x 3.5 cm height)

Line muffin pan with paper cases.

Sift plain flour, baking powder and bicarbonate of soda together.

In bowl of electric cake mixer, cream butter and castor sugar until light and creamy. Beat in egg for 1 minute until light and fluffy.

Pour in condensed milk and mix well. Fold in sifted ingredients. Stir in jackfruit.

Spoon mixture evenly into cases and level surfaces with a teaspoon.

Bake in preheated oven at 175°C for 20–25 minutes until well risen and cake is cooked through when tested with a wooden skewer.

Remove from oven and cool in the pan for 10 minutes before placing on wire rack to cool completely.

Decorate with jackfruit slices.

Makes 10 cupcakes

Papaya Cupcake with Papaya Glaze Icing

Delight family and friends with this quick and easy tantalizing teatime treat. Choose a bright orange-red ripe Solo papaya for colour and fragrance.

Hi-ratio flour	125 g
Baking powder	1 tsp
Ripe papaya	150 g, peeled and cubed
Butter	85 g, diced
Castor sugar	125 g
Egg	1, large (70 g)
Vanilla essence	$^1/_2$ tsp
Salt	A pinch

Papaya Glaze Icing

Reserved papaya puree	60 g
Lime or lemon juice	2 tsp
Icing sugar	150 g, sifted
Orange food coluring	A tiny drop

Topping

Fresh white flowers	9, small, brushed with egg white and dusted with castor sugar
Large paper cases	9 (5 cm base x 3.5 cm height)

Line muffin pan with paper cases.

Sift hi-ratio flour and baking powder together.

Place papaya cubes in an electric chopper bowl and puree until smooth. Reserve 75 g of puree for the cakes.

Pass the remaining puree through a fine sieve, pressing down with back of a metal spoon to make a fine puree without lumps. There should be 60 g of fine puree for the icing.

In a mixing bowl, cream the butter and sugar until light and fluffy. Beat in the egg for about 1 minute. Then, beat in essence and salt.

Fold in sifted ingredients alternately with 75 g of the papaya puree.

Spoon mixture evenly to fill paper cases. Level surfaces with a teaspoon and make a slight hollow in the centres.

Bake in preheated oven at 175°C for 20 minutes or until cooked through when tested with a wooden skewer.

Meanwhile, prepare papaya glaze icing. Place fine papaya puree and lime juice in a small heatproof saucepan over medium heat. Stir until just beginning to bubble. Stir in sugar and orange colouring until icing is smooth and thick.

Cool cakes in the pan. Cover with papaya glaze icing and decorate if desired.

Makes 9 cupcakes

Note: Hi-ratio flour is milled from low-protein wheat flour. This flour has a high absorbency for liquid, sugar and fat, hence the term 'high-ratio'. Cakes made from this flour have good volume, tender crumbs and very fine texture.

Fruity Carrot Raisin Cupcake

With carrots and raisins, this cupcake has an edgy crunch that will keep you asking for more.

Plain (all-purpose) flour	90 g
Baking powder	$^1/_2$ tsp
Bicarbonate of soda	$^1/_4$ tsp
Mixed spice	$^1/_4$ tsp
Butter	90 g, diced
Soft brown sugar	75 g
Eggs	2, medium (60 g each)
Carrot	75 g, grated
Raisins	50 g, coarsely chopped, soaked with 1 Tbsp unsweetened apple juice
Grated lemon rind	1 tsp

Topping

Icing sugar to dust	
Marzipan carrots	
Medium paper cases	9

Grease sides and line bases of 9 muffin pans with rounds of non-stick paper.

Sift plain flour, baking powder, bicarbonate of soda and mixed spice together.

Cream the butter and sugar until light and fluffy. Beat in the eggs one at a time.

Stir in grated carrot, raisin mixture and sifted ingredients.

Fill prepared muffin pans evenly with mixture. Level surfaces with the back of a teaspoon.

Bake in preheated oven at 175°C for 20–25 minutes.

Cool in the pans before removing onto a wire rack. Transfer to paper cases. Serve dusted with icing sugar and decorated with marzipan carrots.

Makes 9 cupcakes

Note: If desired, place the cakes in paper cases and decorate with cream cheese icing and top with baby marzipan carrots.

Peach Cupcakes

This tantalising yet simple peach cupcake is a definite hit with the kids.

Self-raising flour	125 g
Ground almonds	30 g
Butter	180 g
Castor sugar	140 g
Grated orange rind	From 1 orange
Vanilla essence	$^1/_4$ tsp
Eggs	3, large (70 g each)
Canned peach halves	3–4, diced
Poppy or sesame seeds	1 Tbsp (10 g), toasted
Medium paper cases	24 (4.5 cm base x 2.5 cm height)

Put 2 oven racks on the lowest rack and third rack from the bottom of the oven. Preheat oven to 170°C (fan-oven).

Line two 12-hole patty tins with 24 paper cases.

Sift self-raising flour and ground almonds together.

Cream butter and castor sugar until light and fluffy. Put in grated orange rind and vanilla essence.

Add eggs one at a time, beating well after each addition. Gently fold in the sifted flour and ground almonds, peaches and poppy or sesame seeds.

Spoon mixture into paper cases to fill up to three-quarters full. Place trays on the two oven racks.

Bake at 170°C for 18–20 minutes, switching the trays halfway through baking time, until cakes are cooked through and lightly browned.

Cool in the trays for 10 minutes before transferring onto wire racks to cool completely.

Makes 24 cupcakes

Fruit and Nut Cupcakes

Banana Passionfruit Pecan Cupcake

An exceptional cupcake recipe with the sweet and tangy flavour of passionfruit.

Butter	**65 g, diced**
Castor sugar	**80 g**
Egg	**1, small (55 g)**
Ripe bananas	**90 g, peeled and mashed**
Pecans or walnuts	**20 g, coarsely chopped**
Yoghurt	**65 ml**
Passionfruit pulp	**1 Tbsp**
Self-raising flour	**125 g, sifted**

Passionfruit Icing

Icing sugar	**125 g, sifted**
Passionfruit pulp	**35 g**

Topping

**Extra passionfruit pulp
for decoration**

Large paper cases	**8 (5.5 cm base x 3.5 cm height)**

Line muffin tray with paper cases.

Cream butter and sugar until light and fluffy. Beat in the egg for 1 minute. Stir in mashed bananas, pecans, yoghurt and passionfruit pulp. Fold in flour.

Spoon batter evenly into paper cases and level with a teaspoon.

Bake in preheated oven at 175°C for 30 minutes or until cooked through when tested with a wooden skewer.

Prepare passion fruit icing by placing icing sugar into a heatproof bowl and stirring in the passion fruit pulp to form a stiff paste.

Stand bowl over simmering water and stir until icing is of a pouring consistency. Do not overheat.

Spoon and spread icing over hot cakes. Top with extra passionfruit pulp.

Makes 8 cupcakes

Note: Prepare the icing as soon as cupcakes are removed from the oven and use immediately. It is easier to spread the icing on hot cakes otherwise the icing will thicken and set too quickly.

Banana Pistachio Cupcake

A soft, warm cake with a nutty flavour, perfect for enjoying a late afternoon tea.

Vegetable shortening	**30 g**
Butter	**30 g, diced**
Castor sugar	**110 g**
Vanilla essence	**1 tsp**
Salt	**$^1/_4$ tsp**
Egg	**1, large (70 g)**
Self-raising flour	**120 g**
Bicarbonate of soda	**$^1/_2$ tsp**
Ripe bananas	**300 g, peeled and mashed**
Whipping cream	**1 Tbsp**
Pistachio nuts	**30 g, chopped**

Topping

Red glace cherries	**9**
Icing sugar to dust (optional)	

Large paper cases	**9 (5.5 cm base x 3.5 cm height)**

Cream vegetable shortening, butter and castor sugar until light and fluffy. Beat in essence, salt and egg until well combined.

Sift self-raising flour and bicarbonate of soda together. Fold in sifted ingredients and stir in cream. Add banana and nuts, and mix well.

Spoon mixture evenly into paper cases and level the surfaces. Place a cherry on the centre of each cupcake.

Bake in preheated oven at 175°C for 30 minutes until surface is golden brown or cake is cooked through when tested with a wooden skewer.

Cool cake in pan for 10 minutes before removing onto a wire rack to cool completely.

Serve lightly dusted with icing sugar, if desired.

Makes 9 cupcakes

Orange Marzipan Cupcake

This cupcake looks absolutely appetising with bright orange toppings.

Self-raising flour	**100 g**
Baking powder	**1/2 tsp**
Butter	**100 g, at room temperature**
Castor sugar	**100 g**
Eggs	**3, medium (60–65 g each), separated**
Marzipan	**40 g, chopped into fine crumbles (recipe on page 151)**
Grated orange rind	**1 tsp**
Fresh orange juice	**2 Tbsp**

Topping

Candied orange slices	**12 (recipe on page 151)**
Large paper cases	**12 (4.5 cm base x 3.5 cm height)**

Line a 12-hole muffin pan with paper cases.

Sift self-raising flour and baking powder together.

Cream butter and sugar in bowl of an electric cake mixer until light and creamy. Beat in the egg yolks, one at a time, until mixture is thick.

Fold in sifted ingredients, the marzipan crumbs, orange rind and juice.

Whisk egg white in a separate bowl until just stiff and fold into the butter mixture, one-third at a time.

Spoon mixture evenly into paper cases and level surfaces with the back of a teaspoon.

Bake in preheated oven at 170°C (fan oven) for 8 minutes. Carefully slide muffin pan halfway out of oven and place a candied orange slice on top of each cake.

Continue baking for a further 12 minutes or until cooked through when tested with a wooden skewer. Remove and leave to cool in the pan.

Makes 12 cupcakes

Note: Candied Orange Slices are quick and easy to make and they store well in a covered container in the refrigerator for 4–6 weeks. Glossy, sweet and zesty, they make attractive decorations for cheesecakes, fruity cakes, flans and jellies. You can also stamp out flower patterns or cut the peels into strips to make candied peels and use as toppings. For cut-out florets or peel strips, pare off some of the white pith from quartered orange peel and follow the recipe on page 151.

Orange Craisin Banana Cupcake

This is delicious and it has many different textures to tickle the taste buds. Use Del Monte bananas and Tia Maria for the best results.

Butter	**100 g, diced**
Castor sugar	**80 g**
Egg	**1, large (70 g)**
Grated orange rind	**1 tsp**
Orange juice	**1 Tbsp**
Self-raising flour	**85 g, sifted**
Ripe bananas	**210 g, peeled and mashed**
Craisins	**40 g, 9 g reserved for topping and remainder coarsely chopped**

Topping

Almond flakes for sprinkling	**15 g**
Large paper cases	**9 (5.5 cm base x 3.5 cm height)**

Cream butter and castor sugar until light and fluffy. Beat in the egg for 1 minute and add orange rind and juice.

Fold in flour alternately with mashed bananas. Stir in craisins.

Spoon mixture evenly into paper cases and level the surfaces.

Sprinkle with almond flakes and place a craisin on the centre of each cupcake.

Bake in preheated oven at 175°C for 25 minutes or until cooked through when tested with a wooden skewer.

Makes 9 cupcakes

Note: Craisins are sweetened dried cranberries, wrinkled and dark red in colour. They can be used mixed with cereals or in cookies, muffins, pancakes and breads. They are easily available in leading supermarkets.

Mango Walnut Crumble Cupcake

This is wonderful with a crunchy walnut topping.

Cold butter	**90 g, diced**
Castor sugar	**80 g**
Eggs	**2, medium (65 g each)**
Grated orange rind	**1 tsp**
Self-raising flour	**90 g, sifted**
Milk	**1 Tbsp**
Mango flesh	**80 g, cut into 2.5 x 1.5-cm pieces**
Crumble Topping	
Gingernut biscuits	**60 g**
Walnuts	**15 g**
Melted butter	**30 g**
Paper cases	**10 (4 cm base x 3 cm height)**

Line patty tin with paper cases.

Prepare crumble topping by processing biscuits and walnuts until finely crushed. Add butter and process for a few seconds until just combined. Set aside.

Cream butter and castor sugar until light and fluffy. Beat in eggs, one at a time and beating well after each addition, and orange rind. Add flour and milk and mix well.

Fill paper cases half-full with batter. Press mango into the batter. Spread batter to cover mango with a teaspoon and level the surfaces. Sprinkle two teaspoons of crumble topping on top of each cupcake.

Bake in preheated oven at 190°C for 15 minutes or until topping is browned and a skewer inserted into the centre of the cake comes out clean.

Makes 10 cupcakes

Apple Almond Dessert Cupcake

A quick and easy dessert to prepare for entertaining buffet style.

Green apples	**2 (approximately 130 g each), peeled, cored and cut into 1-cm cubes**
Demerara sugar	**15 g**
Grated lemon rind	**From ½ a lemon**
Lemon juice	**¹/₂ Tbsp**
Butter	**90 g**
Castor sugar	**75 g**
Egg	**1, large (70 g), beaten with a fork**
Self-raising flour	**75 g, sifted**
Ground almonds	**75 g**
Grated lemon rind	**From ½ a lemon**
Milk	**3–4 Tbsp**

Topping
Almond flakes for sprinkling

Large paper cases	**12 (5 cm base x 3.5 cm height)**

Line muffin pan with paper cases.

Combine apples, sugar, lemon rind and juice in a bowl. Mix well and set aside.

Cream butter and sugar until light and creamy. Beat in the egg until light and fluffy.

Fold in sifted flour, ground almonds, lemon rind and milk to give a soft dropping consistency.

Divide apples evenly into prepared cases. Spoon and spread mixture evenly over the apples. Sprinkle with some almond flakes.

Bake in preheated oven at 175°C for 20–30 minutes or until cooked through when tested with a wooden skewer.

Cool cakes in the pan.

Makes 12 cupcakes

Jackfruit Almond Cupcake

This cupcake is moist, fragrant and scrumptious. It can be served warm or at room temperature.

Seedless fragrant jackfruit	**200 g, cut into 1-cm cubes**
Brown sugar	**15 g**
Butter	**120 g, at room temperature**
Castor sugar	**100 g**
Eggs	**2, large (70 g each), beaten with a fork**
Ground almonds	**120 g**
Topping	
Almond flakes for sprinkling	**15 g**
Large paper cases	**12 (5.5 cm base x 3.5 cm height)**

Line muffin tray with paper cases.

Combine jackfruit and brown sugar in a mixing bowl. Stir to mix evenly and set aside.

Cream butter and sugar until light and creamy. Gradually beat in eggs, one at a time. Fold in ground almonds.

Divide jackfruit evenly and spread on base of paper cases.

Spoon almond mixture evenly to cover jackfruit and level surfaces with the back of a teaspoon. Sprinkle some almond flakes on top of each cake.

Bake in preheated oven at 175°C for 23–25 minutes or until cooked through when tested with a wooden skewer.

Cool cakes in the pan.

Makes 12 cupcakes

Plain (all-purpose) flour	85 g
Baking powder	$^1/_2$ tsp
Hazelnuts	35 g
Pear halves	180 g, drained weight, from 1 can (410 g) pear halves
Butter	75 g, diced
Castor sugar	90 g
Grated lemon rind	1 tsp
Egg	1, large (70 g)
Vanilla essence	$^1/_2$ tsp
Low-fat milk	45 ml
Pear syrup	$^1/_2$ Tbsp, from the can
Large paper cases	9 (4.5 m base x 3.5 cm height)

Hazelnut Pear Cupcakes

The sweet taste of pears gives a rustic feel to this light cupcake.

Line muffin pan with paper cases.

Sift flour and baking powder together.

Place hazelnuts in a small chopper bowl and blend finely. Reserve one-third portion for topping. Sprinkle 1 tspful of topping into each paper case from the remainder.

Slice pears into 0.75-cm thick slices and cut each slice into two pieces. Place 3 pieces into each paper case over the hazelnuts. Reserve 9 pieces for topping.

Cream butter, sugar and lemon rind until light and creamy. Beat in egg and vanilla essence until well combined.

Stir in milk and fold in sifted ingredients. Lastly, stir in pear syrup.

Spoon mixture evenly into cases. Use a teaspoon to level the surfaces and press a piece of reserved pear halfway into the centre of each cake. Sprinkle some ground hazelnuts on top.

Bake in preheated oven at 175°C for 25 minutes or until cake is cooked through when tested with a wooden skewer.

Remove from oven and stand cakes in the pan for 15 minutes before placing on wire rack to cool completely.

Makes 9 cupcakes

Hot Island Orange Almond Cupcake

A popular favourite for either breakfast or dessert.

Sweet orange marmalade	125 g
Butter	45 g
Eggs	3, large (70 g each), separated
Grated orange rind	1½ tsp
Castor sugar	110 g
Orange juice or Drambuie	2 Tbsp
Ground almonds	105 g
Self-raising flour	1 Tbsp (5 g)
Madeleine tins	8
Medium paper cases	8

Grease sides and line base of 8 madeleine tins with greased greaseproof paper.

Combine marmalade and butter in a small saucepan. Stir over heat, without boiling, until marmalade is dissolved.

Boil, uncovered, for about 1 minute just to thicken the sauce slightly. Spoon about 2 tspfuls od sauce into each prepared cup.

Put egg yolks and rind into bowl of an electric cake mixer fitted with a beater. Whisk with half of the sugar (55 g) until pale and creamy.

Stir in the orange juice and ground almonds. Fold in self-raising flour.

Whisk egg whites in a separate bowl with remaining sugar until soft peaks form.

Fold egg white mixture into egg yolk mixture and spoon into prepared tins (about 2 Tbspful).

Place tins on oven tray and bake in preheated moderate oven at 175°C for 25 minutes.

Turn cakes out immediately and place in paper cases. Serve preferably warm with a scoop of fresh cream.

Makes 8 cupcakes

Note: For those who dislike bitter marmalade jam, use sweet orange marmalade from IXL brand which is not bitter as the marmalade is made from fresh Australian navel oranges using the orange peel without the pith.

Durian Hazelnut Cupcake

This is a creamy cupcake with a delicate Asian flavour of durians.

Self-raising flour	**125 g**
Baking powder	**$^1/_2$ tsp**
Bicarbonate of soda	**$^1/_2$ tsp**
Salt	**A pinch**
Castor sugar	**100 g**
Cold butter	**120 g, diced**
Good quality durian pulp	**120 g**
Low-fat milk	**35 ml**
Egg	**1, large (70 g), beaten with a fork**
Hazelnuts	**30 g, coarsely chopped**

Topping

Toasted black sesame seeds for sprinkling

Large paper cases	**10 (5 cm base x 3.5 cm height)**

Sift self-raising flour, baking powder and bicarbonate of soda together.

Place sifted ingredients and salt into a food processor. Stir in castor sugar. Add cold butter and blend until mixture is crumbly.

Place durian pulp in a bowl of a small food processor or chopper bowl fitted with a cutting blade. Add milk and blend into a fine puree.

Pour durian puree into butter mixture. Add the beaten egg and blend until well combined. Stir in hazelnuts.

Spoon mixture evenly to fill the paper cases up to two-thirds full. Level surfaces with the back of a teaspoon.

Bake in preheated oven at 175°C for 20–22 minutes or until golden brown in colour.

Remove cakes from the oven and sprinkle with some black sesame seeds.

Makes 10 cupcakes

Note: Use good quality ripe fragrant durian pulp and you will be rewarded with a light, moist fragrant cupcake with a tender texture.

Upside-Down Caramel Pineapple Cupcake

A cupcake version of an all-time favourite.

Self-raising flour	**120 g**
Baking powder	**1 tsp**
Butter	**60 g**
Brown sugar	**35 g**
Rum or pineapple syrup from the can	**1 Tbsp**
Canned pineapple rings	**12, from 2 cans (234 g each)**
Glace cherries	**6, halved**
Cold butter	**125 g, diced**
Castor sugar	**90 g**
Vanilla essence	**$^1/_2$ tsp**
Eggs	**3, medium (60 g each)**
Milk	**3 Tbsp**
Walnuts	**50 g, coarsely chopped**
Whipped cream for serving	
Large paper cases	**12 (4.5 cm base x 3.5 cm height)**
Medium paper cases	**12 (4 cm by 2.5 cm height)**

Line a 12-hole muffin pan with large white paper cases.

Sift self-raising flour and baking powder together.

Put butter, sugar and rum or pineapple syrup in a small saucepan and cook, stirring until sugar has melted. Simmer for 1–2 minutes. Cool caramel.

Carefully spoon a dessertspoon of caramel into the paper cases. Place a pineapple ring with a cherry half on the centre. Set aside.

Cream butter and sugar with vanilla essence until light and creamy. Add eggs, one at a time, beating well after each addition.

If mixture should curdle, beat in a little of the flour. Fold in remaining sifted ingredients and milk. Stir in walnuts.

Spoon mixture evenly into paper cases over the pineapple slices. Carefully spread mixture to cover pineapple.

Bake in preheated oven at 175°C for 20 minutes or until cooked through when tested with a wooden skewer.

Cool cakes in the pan. Remove, peel off the large paper cases and carefully overturn into the medium paper cases.

Serve with whipped cream.

Makes 12 cupcakes

Note: For this cake, you have to use small pineapple rings, to fit the paper cases. This is available under the Lee Pineapple Brand. The drained weight of a 234 g can is 130 g and there are 7 pineapple rings.

Carrot Pineapple Walnut Cupcake

A fruity and crunchy cupcake that is light and refreshing with a cup of hot tea.

Plain (all-purpose) flour	150 g
Baking powder	1 tsp
Bicarbonate of soda	$^3/_4$ tsp
Ground cinnamon	$^1/_2$ tsp
Eggs	2, large (75 g each), lightly beaten with a fork
Sunflower oil	100 ml
Carrot	200 g, grated
Fresh ripe pineapple	120 g coarsely chopped and drained
Castor sugar	130 g
Walnuts	40 g, chopped

Cream Cheese Icing

Butter	120 g
Cream cheese	120 g, at room temperature
Vanilla essence	$^1/_2$ tsp
Icing sugar	110 g, sifted

Topping

Baby marzipan carrots to decorate	(Marzipan recipe on page 151)
Large paper cases	12 (5.5 cm base x 3.5 cm height)

Line muffin pan with paper cases.

Sift flour, baking powder, bicarbonate of soda and ground cinnamon together.

Beat eggs and oil together in bowl of an electric cake mixer fitted with a beater for 1 minute. Add sifted ingredients, carrot, pineapple and sugar. Beat for 1 minute. Stir in walnuts.

Fill the paper cases evenly with the mixture up to two-thirds full and level surfaces with the back of a teaspoon.

Bake in preheated oven at 175°C for 30–35 minutes or until cooked through when tested with a wooden skewer.

Remove cakes from oven and cool in the pan for 10 minutes. Then place on a wire rack to cool completely.

Prepare cream cheese icing by placing butter, cream cheese and vanilla essence in a mixing bowl and beat until light and creamy. Add icing sugar and beat again until light and smooth.

Spread cream cheese icing on each cupcake. Decorate with baby marzipan carrots, if desired.

Makes 12 cupcakes

Mango Jelly Cupcake

This is an elegant and delicious cupcake which combines the softness of a cake and the smoothness of jelly. Perfect for all ages.

Ripe mango	1, medium, peeled and sliced, 200 g net weight
Self-raising flour	125 g
Ground almonds	30 g
Butter	180 g
Light brown sugar	160 g
Grated lemon rind	From 1 lemon
Vanilla essence	¹/₄ tsp
Eggs	3, large (70 g each)
Poppy seeds	1 Tbsp (10 g)
Topping	
Agar agar powder	1 tsp (2 g)
Water	200 ml
Sugar	45 g
Reserved mango puree	100 g, combined with 2 tsp lemon juice
Thinly sliced mango strips for decoration	
Large paper cases	12 (5.5 cm base x 4 cm height)

Dice 100 g of mango and puree remaining 100 g for jelly topping.

Sift self-raising flour and ground almonds together.

Cream butter, sugar, lemon rind and vanilla essence until light and fluffy. Add eggs, one at a time, beating well after each addition.

Gently fold in sifted ingredients and the poppy seeds.

Spoon batter into paper cases, dividing it evenly. Put about 3 pieces of mango in the centre of each cake.

Bake in preheated oven at 190°C for about 20–23 minutes or until surface is golden and a skewer inserted into the centre comes out clean.

Remove from oven and place on a wire rack.

Make jelly topping by putting agar agar powder, water and sugar into a small saucepan and bring to a boil. Continue to boil, stirring until the agar agar powder is dissolved completely.

Pour in pureed mango mixture and bring to a gentle boil.

Cool a little and spoon over the cakes to cover completely. Allow to set and serve at room temperature. Decorate with thin mango strips.

Makes 12 cupcakes

Note: The mango slices will sink in during baking time. Poppy seeds can be replaced with toasted sesame seeds.

Mango Streusel Cupcake

Tastes simply wonderful and doesn't require a lot of time to do. The streusel gives an added nutty taste.

Butter	**90 g**
Castor sugar	**80 g**
Eggs	**2, medium (65 g each)**
Grated lemon rind	**1 tsp**
Self-raising flour	**90 g, sifted**
Low-fat milk	**1 Tbsp**
Ripe mangoes	**120 g, peeled and cut into 3 x 1 x 0.5-cm thick slices**

Streusel

Cold butter	**20 g, cubed**
Plain (all-purpose) flour	**25 g, sifted**
Demerara sugar	**1 Tbsp**
Hazelnuts	**20 g, toasted and chopped**
Large paper cases	**10 (5 cm base x 3.5 cm height)**

Line muffin tray with paper cases.

Cream butter and castor sugar until light and fluffy using an electric hand-held mixer. Gradually beat in the eggs, one at a time.

Beat in the lemon rind. Fold in flour followed by milk.

Spoon mixture evenly to fill paper cases and level with a teaspoon.

Arrange about 3 slices of mangoes on top of each cake. Sprinkle 1 teaspoonful streusel over mangoes.

Bake in preheated oven at 190°C for 20 minutes until light golden in colour and cooked through when tested with a wooden skewer.

* To Prepare Streusel

Place cold butter cubes, flour and sugar in bowl of a small food chopper or processor. Process in spurts until mixture becomes crumbly.

Add hazelnuts and process a couple of seconds until mixture is like coarse breadcrumbs.

Makes 10 cupcakes

Note: It is essential that the butter is really cold or the mixture will become lumpy when processed. If this should happen, place chopper bowl in the freezer for about 10–15 minutes and then process again.

Photo on page 100-101

Swedish Apple Cupcake

This is a moist and light cake with a refreshingly lemony tart apple on the base. The recipe calls for a few more steps, but the result is definitely worth the effort.

Green apple	1, peeled, quartered and cored
Lemon juice	½ Tbsp
Castor sugar	100 g
Butter	100 g, diced
Eggs	2, medium (60–65 g each), separated
Ground almonds	100 g
Grated lemon rind	From 1 lemon
Lemon juice	1 Tbsp
Topping	
Almond nips for sprinkling	15 g
Whipped cream or ice-cream to serve	
Large paper cases	9 (5.5 cm base x 3.5 cm height)

Line muffin pan with paper cases.

Slice the apple into 20 thin slices and arrange on the base of the paper cases.

Sprinkle each paper case with lemon juice and a pinch of castor sugar.

Cream butter with remaining castor sugar until light and fluffy. Beat in egg yolks, followed by the almonds, lemon rind and juice.

Whisk the egg whites until they are just stiff. Mix one-third of the egg white into the mixture and fold gently to slacken the batter. Fold in remaining egg whites carefully.

Spoon mixture into the paper cases with the apples. Level the surfaces and sprinkle some almond nips on top of each cupcake.

Bake in preheated oven at 175°C for 25 minutes or until top is golden brown.

Remove from oven and serve cupcakes either warm or cold with whipped cream or ice-cream.

Makes 9 cupcakes

Banana Date and Nut Cupcake

A simple cupcake recipe for a lazy, relaxing weekend.

Self-raising flour	120 g
Bicarbonate of soda	½ tsp
Butter	125 g
Caster sugar	120 g
Eggs	2 (65 g each)
Ripe banana	1, large (approximately 120 g without skin), mashed
Fresh grated white coconut	50 g
Milk	1 Tbsp
Seedless dates	4, large, each sliced into 4 strips and flattened with a flat knife
Almond slices	15 g
Medium paper cases	15 (4 cm base x 2 cm height)

Line patty tins with the paper cases.

Sift self-raising flour and bicarbonate of soda together.

In a mixing bowl, cream the butter and sugar until light and fluffy. Add eggs, one at a time, and beat until well combined.

Stir in mashed bananas. Fold in sifted flour and coconut and stir in milk.

Spoon mixture evenly into the paper cases to three-quarters full. Place a slice of flattened date on surface and sprinkle over some almond slices.

Bake in preheated oven at 175°C (fan oven) for 15 minutes or until cooked through.

Cool cakes in the pan for 10 minutes before removing onto a wire rack to cool.

Makes 15 cupcakes

Note: If you have ready packaged seedless dates with almonds, simply cut into slices and place on top of each cupcake.

Rich Almond Semolina Cupcake

This cupcake uses only semolina and ground almonds in place of flour. It has a wonderful light texture with moist centre.

Butter	**90 g, diced**
Castor sugar	**45 g**
Salt	**A pinch**
Rum or any fresh fruit juice	**2 tsp**
Vanilla essence	**$^1/_2$ tsp**
Evaporated milk	**25 ml**
Egg yolks	**3, medium (from eggs weighing 60 g each)**
Castor sugar	**20 g**
Semolina	**35 g**
Ground almonds	**30 g**
Egg whites	**2, medium**
Cream of tartar	**A pinch**
Castor sugar	**15 g**
Topping	
Coconut slivers	**15 g, toasted**
Large paper cases	**10 (5 cm base x 3.5 cm height)**

Line muffin pan with paper cases.

Cream butter and castor sugar in a mixing bowl until light and fluffy. Beat in salt, rum, essence and evaporated milk.

In a small jug or bowl, using an electric hand-held whisk, beat egg yolks and sugar until light pale and thick.

Combine semolina and ground almonds and fold into the egg yolk mixture. Then on lowest speed, fold this mixture into the butter mixture, one-third at a time.

In a separate bowl, whisk egg whites with cream of tartar until soft peaks form. Beat in sugar until mixture is just stiff.

Fold egg white mixture into main mixture, one half at a time.

Spoon mixture evenly into the paper cases and level with a teaspoon. Top with toasted coconut slivers.

Bake in preheated oven at 160°C for 15 minutes. Reduce heat to 150°C and continue to bake for a further 12–15 minutes until golden brown in colour.

Makes 10 cupcakes

Spice Cupcakes

Apple Cupcake with Cinnamon Apple Topping

Apples and cinnamon are always a surefire combination.

Butter	**125 g, at room temperature**
Castor sugar	**90 g**
Vanilla essence	**1 tsp**
Eggs	**2, large (70 g each)**
Self-raising flour	**180g, sifted**
Low-fat milk	**75 ml**
Green apples	**2 (about 125 g each), peeled, cored and grated into shreds**

Topping

Reserved shredded apple	
Ground cinnamon	**$^1/_2$ tsp, combined and mixed well with 1 Tbsp castor sugar**
Butter	**20 g, well-chilled and diced pea-sized**
Large paper cases	**10 (5 cm base by 3.5 cm height)**

Line muffin pan with paper cases.

Use an electric cake mixer to cream butter, sugar and vanilla essence until light and fluffy. Beat in eggs, one at a time until well combined.

Fold in flour alternately with milk.

Lightly squeeze shredded apples between hands to remove some apple juice. Stir 2 tablespoons apple juice and 25g shredded apples into flour mixture. Reserve remaining shredded apples for topping.

Spoon mixture evenly into prepared paper cases and level surfaces with the back of a teaspoon.

Sprinkle remaining shredded apples over top of cakes. Sprinkle combined cinnamon and sugar over apples. Put some butter cubes on top of apples.

Bake in preheated oven at 175°C for 25 minutes or until cooked through when tested with a wooden skewer and topping is browned.

Makes 10 cupcakes

Note: When cold butter is cut into tiny pieces in hot weather, it softens very quickly making it rather difficult to handle. To prevent this, place the cubed butter in the freezer compartment before making the cakes.

Eversoft Ginger and Spice

A light moist ginger cake that is easily whipped up using only hand-held balloon whisk.

Plain (all-purpose) flour	**90 g**
Self-raising flour	**30 g**
Bicarbonate of soda	**$^1/_2$ tsp**
Ground ginger	**1 tsp**
Cinnamon powder	**$^1/_4$ tsp**
Mixed spice	**$^1/_4$ tsp**
Castor sugar	**80 g**
Egg	**1, large (70 g), combined with $^1/_2$ cup milk**
Butter	**60 g, at room temperature**
Treacle	**100 g**
Golden syrup	**25 g**
Topping	
Candied ginger	
Sesame seeds for sprinkling	**1 heaped tsp, toasted**
Large paper cases	**10 (5 cm base by 3.75 cm height)**

Line a muffin pan with paper cases and set aside. Preheat oven to 175°C (fan oven).

Sift plain and self-raising flour, bicarbonate of soda, ground ginger, cinnamon powder and mixed spice into a large mixing bowl and stir in sugar.

Lightly whisk combined egg and milk with a hand-held balloon whisk for 30 seconds and add to dry ingredients. Stir to mix well with the balloon whisk.

Place butter, treacle and golden syrup in a small non-stick saucepan. Stir constantly over gentle heat, just to melt the butter.

Stir warm mixture into the flour mixture.

Fill the paper cases with the runny batter, each up to three-quarters full. Bake in preheated oven for 20 minutes or until well risen and a wooden skewer inserted in the centre of the cake comes out clean.

Cool in the tin for 5 minutes before removing onto a wire rack to cool completely.

Decorate with candied ginger and sprinkle some sesame seeds on surface of each cupcake.

Makes 10 cupcakes

Note: To prevent treacle or golden syrup from sticking to the spoon, either dip spoon in boiling hot water or lightly grease the front of the spoon with butter. The treacle or golden syrup will slide off the spoon easily.

Spiced Fruity Cupcake with Almond Paste

Almond Paste

Castor sugar	**200 g**
Almonds	**200 g, finely ground**
Egg	**1, medium (65 g), lightly beaten with a fork**
Lemon juice	**¹/₂ Tbsp**

Cake Mixture

Butter	**115 g**
Brown sugar	**110 g**
Mixed dried fruit	**250 g, chopped if fruits are in large pieces**
Dried apricots	**50 g, chopped**
Glace cherries	**50 g, rinsed, drained and chopped**
Grated orange or lemon rind	**From 1 orange or lemon**
Orange or lemon juice	**60 ml**
Brandy or extra orange juice	**2 Tbsp**
Almonds	**50 g, toasted and chopped**
Self-raising flour	**175 g**
Ground mixed spice	**1 tsp**
Freshly grated nutmeg	**¹/₄ tsp**
Eggs	**2, large (70 g each), beaten with an electric hand whisk**
Apricot jam	**1 Tbsp, dissolved in 1 Tbsp brandy or water**
Large paper cases	**12 (5.5 cm base x 3.5 cm height)**

* To Prepare Almond Paste (a day ahead)

Place sugar and almonds in food processor and blend for a few seconds. Add beaten egg and lemon juice and blend until combined.

Remove from bowl and knead into a firm ball. Place in a plastic bag, flatten into a small rectangle and refrigerate overnight for use.

* To Prepare Cake Mixture (a day ahead)

Put cake mixture ingredients except toasted almonds into a medium non-stick saucepan and heat gently, stirring until butter has melted. Simmer for 2–3 seconds.

Remove and stir in almonds. Cool, cover and leave overnight to absorb liquid.

* To Make Cupcakes

On baking day, roll out 12 pieces (5 g each) of almond paste into a ball and flatten each into a disc.

Roll out remaining paste, between plastic sheets, to about 0.4-cm thick. Use a floral 5.5-cm cookie cutter to cut out 12 floral rounds for topping. Set aside.

Sift self-raising flour, mixed spice and grated nutmeg.

Place cake mixture into bowl of an electric mixer. Add sifted ingredients and mix on lowest speed until just combined. Fold in beaten eggs.

Line a muffin pan with paper cases. Spoon half the mixture evenly into the prepared cases. Lightly press an almond paste disc on top. Spoon remaining mixture over the almond paste and smoothen the surfaces with a teaspoon.

Bake in preheated oven at 150°C for 35 minutes or until golden brown and cooked through when tested with a wooden skewer.

Remove from oven, brush surfaces with the apricot mixture and top each cake with a floral almond paste piece.

Grill in a preheated grill for 3 minutes or until golden brown.

Makes 12 cupcakes

Spice Streusel and Apricot Cupcake

Sweetness and spiciness all rolled into one in this wonderfully delicious cupcake.

Streusel

Plain (all-purpose) flour	**30 g, sifted**
Dark brown sugar	**50 g**
Cold butter	**30 g, diced**
Ground cinnamon	**$^1/_2$ tsp**
Nutmeg powder	**$^1/_4$ tsp**

Batter

Plain (all-purpose) flour	**175 g**
Baking powder	**$^3/_4$ tsp**
Bicarbonate of soda	**$^1/_2$ tsp**
Salt	**$^1/_4$ tsp**
Butter	**105 g**
Granulated sugar	**120 g**
Vanilla essence	**$^1/_2$ tsp**
Almond essence	**$^1/_4$ tsp**
Eggs	**2, large (70–75 g each)**
Cream	**120 ml**
Lemon juice	**1 tsp**
Dried apricots	**75 g, chopped**

Lemon Glaze Icing

Icing sugar	**110 g, sifted**
Lemon juice	**$1^1/_2$ Tbsp**

Muffin pans	**10**
Large paper cases	**10**

Prepare the streusel, place flour, sugar, butter and spices into a small electric chopper bowl and pulse until mixture turns crumbly. Set aside.

Sift plain flour, baking powder and bicarbonate of soda together and add salt. Set aside.

Prepare the batter. Cream the butter, sugar and essences for 1–2 minutes. Beat in the eggs, one at a time. Add sifted ingredients and beat again, gradually adding cream at the same time. Stir in lemon juice and apricots.

Grease 10 muffin pans with butter or spray with canned spray oil.

Spoon half of the batter into the prepared pans. Level surfaces with a teaspoon.

Sprinkle a teaspoonful of streusel over the batter. Spoon remaining batter over streusel and smoothen the surfaces.

Bake in preheated oven at 175°C for 25 minutes or until golden and cooked through when tested with a wooden skewer.

Cool cupcakes for 10 minutes before inverting over a wire rack. Place them in paper cases.

Meanwhile, prepare lemon glaze icing. Put lemon juice in a small bowl and microwave on high for 15 seconds until bubbling hot. Stir into icing sugar until combined and smooth.

Spoon icing into a piping bag fitted with a writing nozzle. Pipe criss-cross lines across surface of each cupcake.

Makes 10 cupcakes

Note: When putting streusel ingredients together, ensure that the butter is really cold or else the ingredients will clump together. If this should happen, place the bowl in the freezer for about 15 minutes to harden. Then pulse again into fine crumbs.

Ginger Date and Apple Cupcake

This is a moist cupcake made with fresh ginger that will keep well for 3–4 days in an airtight container in the refrigerator. It is great served slightly warmed. Heat in a microwave for 15–20 seconds.

Dates	**100 g, pitted and chopped coarsely**
Boiling water	**100 ml**
Butter	**100 g, diced**
Dark brown sugar	**125 g**
Egg	**1, large (70 g)**
Fresh young ginger	**30 g, peeled and grated**
Grated lemon rind	**1 tsp**
Self-raising flour	**100 g, sifted**
Green apple	**1, small, peeled and diced into 0.5-cm cubes**
Topping	
Dark chocolate	**60 g**
Large paper cases	**12 (5 cm base by 3.5 cm height)**

Line a 12-hole muffin pan with paper cases.

Place dates in a bowl and cover with boiling water. Set aside.

Heat butter in a small saucepan until melted and stir in sugar. Allow to cool.

Add egg and beat for 1 minute. Beat in ginger and lemon rind.

Drain dates and add to main mixture. Mix well. Fold in sifted flour and apple.

Spoon mixture evenly into prepared paper cases and level surfaces with a teaspoon.

Bake in preheated oven at 175°C for 25 minutes or until cooked through when tested with a wooden skewer. Leave to cool in the pan.

Break chocolate into a heatproof bowl over simmering water. Stir until melted and smooth.

Fill a piping bag with a writing nozzle and pipe decoratively on surfaces of cupcakes.

Makes 12 cupcakes

Pumpkin Seed Spice Cupcake with Lime Glaze Icing

An exciting mix of spice and citrus flavours with a crunchy topping.

Plain (all-purpose) flour	**125 g**
Cinnamon powder	³/₄ tsp
All-spice powder	³/₄ tsp
Ground nutmeg	³/₄ tsp
Baking powder	¹/₂ tsp
Bicarbonate of soda	¹/₂ tsp
Butter	**125 g**
Castor sugar	**90 g**
Eggs	**2, medium (60 g each), separated**
Vanilla essence	¹/₂ tsp
Salt	¹/₂ tsp
Natural yoghurt or sour cream	**75 ml**
Pumpkin seeds	**45 g, lightly toasted and coarsely chopped**

Lime Glaze Icing

Icing sugar	**60 g, sifted**
Kalamansi juice	**1 Tbsp**

Topping

Extra toasted pumpkin seeds	

Large paper cases	**12 (4.5 cm base x 3.5 cm height)**

Line a 12-hole muffin pan with paper cases.

Sift plain flour, cinnamon, all-spice powder, nutmeg, baking powder and bicarbonate of soda together.

Cream together butter and castor sugar in bowl of electric mixer until pale and fluffy. Beat in egg yolks, one at a time, and then beat in vanilla essence.

On very low speed, mix in sifted ingredients and salt, alternating with yoghurt or sour cream.

Whisk egg whites in separate bowl until just stiff. Then gently fold into main mixture, half at a time. Mix in pumpkin seeds.

Spoon mixture evenly into the prepared cases and smoothen the surfaces with a teaspoon.

Bake in preheated oven at 175°C for 25 minutes or until cooked through when tested with a wooden skewer.

Cool cupcakes in pan.

Meanwhile, prepare lime glaze icing by placing icing sugar in a mixing bowl. Heat the kalamansi juice in a microwave oven on high for 15–20 seconds. Stir into icing sugar until smooth. Use glaze immediately as it will set very quickly.

Drizzle lime glaze onto cakes and arrange a few pumpkin seeds in the shape of a flower with a pink soft sweet centre.

Makes 12 cupcakes

Note: Pumpkin seeds brown very quickly. Keep an eye on them while toasting. It will only take about 5 minutes in the oven at 175°C.

If candied nutmeg is not available, decorate with toasted pumpkin seeds instead.

Sponge Cupcakes

Angel Food Cupcake with Blueberry Filling

This cupcake is very light and airy and incredibly delicate to the palate. The taste is even more alluring when served with fresh blueberries.

Superfine flour	**125 g**
Icing sugar	**30 g**
Egg whites	**4, large (180 g)**
Salt	**$^1/_4$ tsp**
Vanilla essence	**$^1/_2$ tsp**
Cream of tartar	**$^1/_2$ tsp**
Granulated sugar	**75 g**

Blueberry Filling

Blueberries in heavy syrup	**1 can (425 g), drained**
Granulated sugar	**1 Tbsp**
Blueberry syrup	**3 Tbsp, from the can**
Potato flour	**1 tsp, mixed with 1 Tbsp blueberry syrup**

Butter Glaze Icing

Icing sugar	**160 g, sifted,**
Butter	**30 g, at room temperature**
Lime juice	**2 Tbsp**

Topping

Fresh blueberries

Fruit jam of your choice

Paper cases	**12 (5 cm base x 3.5 cm height)**

Sift superfine flour and icing sugar onto a baking tray and set aside.

In a large mixing bowl attached with a balloon whisk, put in egg whites, salt, vanilla essence and sift in the cream of tartar.

Whisk mixture on high speed until soft peaks form. Gradually beat in the sugar, one-third at a time, until the egg whites are just stiff and glossy.

Sift in half the flour mixture and fold in gently. Sift in remaining flour and fold in lightly until just combined.

Fill the paper cases evenly with the mixture and level surfaces with the back of a teaspoon.

Bake in preheated oven at 160°C for 15 minutes until cakes are springy or cooked through when tested with a wooden skewer.

Meanwhile, prepare the blueberry filling. Puree the drained blueberries and pour into a small saucepan. Stir in sugar and blueberry syrup and bring to a boil. Thicken with potato flour mixture. Cool for use.

Also, prepare the butter glaze icing, place sifted icing sugar in a mixing bowl. Combine butter and lime juice in a heatproof bowl and microwave on high for 1 minute until boiling. Pour gradually into the icing sugar. Stir vigorously until glossy and smooth.

Remove from the oven and cool for 15 minutes. Use a sharp pointed knife or a small cookie cutter (2 cm diameter x 4.5 cm height) to cut out a hole through the cake, taking care not to cut the base paper.

Use a pastry bag fitted with a 0.5-cm plain nozzle and pipe blueberry filling into holes of cupcakes. Cover surface with butter glaze icing. Place a dollop of blueberry filling in the centre. Top with fresh blueberries and drizzle with softened fruit jam.

Makes 12 cupcakes

Apple Cider Vinegar Honey Syrup Sponge Cupcake

This is a soft spongy cupcake made using only fresh white breadcrumbs without flour soaked in a tangy spice-flavoured syrup.

Sponge Batter

Eggs	**2 large (70 g each), separated**
Castor sugar	**80 g, divided into 2 portions**
Grated lemon rind	**1 tsp**
Fresh white fine breadcrumbs	**75 g**

Apple Cider Vinegar Honey Syrup

Apple Cider Vinegar + Honey	**100 ml**
Castor sugar	**40 g**
Orange or apple juice	**2 Tbsp**
Cinnamon stick	**1-cm piece**
Clove	**1 whole piece**
Cointreau	**1 Tbsp, optional**

Topping

Fresh grated white coconut for sprinkling	**1 Tbsp**
Large paper cases	**10 (4.5 cm base x 3.5 cm height)**

Line muffin pans with paper cases.

Place egg yolks with 40 g sugar in bowl of an electric mixer fitted with a balloon whisk. Whisk until pale, thick and light. Beat in lemon rind.

In a separate bowl, whisk egg whites until frothy. Add remaining 40 g of sugar gradually and continue to beat until stiff.

Fold a third of the egg white mixture followed by the breadcrumbs into the egg yolk mixture. Carefully fold in remaining egg white mixture in two batches.

Spoon mixture evenly to fill paper cases and level surfaces with a teaspoon

Bake in preheated oven at 175°C for 15 minutes or until a skewer inserted in the centre of the cake comes out clean.

Cool cakes in pan before taking out.

Meanwhile, prepare Apple Cider Vinegar + Honey syrup. Place all ingredients except Cointreau in a small saucepan and bring to a slow boil. Reduce heat and simmer for 1 minute. Stir in Cointreau if using. Remove and leave spices in the syrup to infuse for 15 minutes.

To serve, spoon about 2 teaspoons of syrup on each cupcake. Sprinkle over with freshly grated white coconut.

Makes 10 cupcakes

Note: This recipe is a good way of using leftover white bread. Simply slice off the crusts and tear them into a food processor. Process until they become fine crumbs. Measure out amount required and use immediately or store in covered containers in the freezer. They will keep for 1–2 months. The 'Apple Cider Vinegar + Honey' is from Wescobee, an Australian product. Cointreau can be replaced with either fresh apple or orange juice.

Coffee Liqueur Chocolate Sponge Cupcake with Chocolate Ganache

Nothing beats the taste of rich coffee-flavoured cake covered with creamy dark chocolate.

Self-raising flour	**75 g**
Cocoa powder	**20 g**
Eggs	**4, large (70 g each)**
Castor sugar	**100 g**
Coffee Syrup	
Low-fat milk	**75 ml**
Coffee liqueur	**1 Tbsp**
Honey	**1 Tbsp**
Chocolate Ganache	
Dark chocolate	**85 g, chopped**
Thickened cream	**30 ml**
Topping	
White chocolate shavings	
Large paper cases	**9 (5 cm base and 3.5 cm height)**

Sift self-raising flour and cocoa powder together.

Place eggs and sugar in the bowl of an electric cake mixer fitted with a balloon whisk and beat on high speed for 5 minutes or until thick and pale.

Fold sifted ingredients, half at a time, into the egg mixture.

Fill the paper cases evenly with the mixture and level surfaces with a teaspoon.

Bake in preheated oven at 175°C for 15 minutes or until cooked through when tested with a wooden skewer.

Meanwhile, combine coffee syrup ingredients in a bowl and stir to dissolve honey.

Remove cakes from oven and prick several holes in each cake with a wooden skewer. Drizzle in a tablespoon of coffee syrup into each cake. Set aside to cool completely.

Meanwhile, prepare chocolate ganache by placing dark chocolate and cream in a bowl over gently simmering water. Stir until chocolate has melted and set aside to cool.

Spread chocolate ganache on each cupcake and top with white chocolate shavings.

Makes 9 cupcakes

Note: For making the perfect light sponge cake, ensure that the eggs are beaten until thick and pale. It should hold the trail of the whisk for 5–6 seconds without sinking in. Fold in sifted flour and cocoa mixture using a large metal spoon. The flour mixture is best sprinkled evenly over the surface of the egg mixture and gently folded in, cutting through the mixture with the edge of the spoon. Work evenly and quickly but without resorting to stirring or worst, beating, which tends to knock out the air from the mixture, which is essential for a good sponge cake.

Almond Sponge Cupcake with Fruity Cream Topping

This cupcake is very pretty especially with the piped cream edges.

Sponge Batter

Marzipan	**25 g (recipe on page 151)**
Ground almonds	**15 g**
Eggs	**3, medium (60 g each), separated**
Castor sugar	**70 g, divided into 2 portions of 50 g and 20 g each**
Vanilla essence	**¹/₂ tsp**
Plain (all-purpose) flour	**25 g, sifted**

Fruit Topping

Orange juice	**6 Tbsp**
Pineapple	**200 g, fresh or canned, cut into small wedges**
Kiwi fruit	**2, peeled and cut into 12 slices**
Whipping cream	**150 ml, chilled**
Large paper cases	**12 (6 cm base x 3.5 cm height)**

Grease sides and line bases of a 12-hole muffin pan with non-stick paper.

Place marzipan and ground almonds in a small chopper or food processor and blend into fine crumbs. Set aside.

Whisk the egg yolks with 50 g of the castor sugar in bowl of an electric cake mixer fitted with a balloon whisk until pale and thick.

Fold in vanilla essence and the marzipan/almond mixture. Sift flour over the mixture and fold with mixer on lowest speed or with a large metal spoon.

Whisk the egg whites in a separate bowl until just beginning to stiffen. Add remaining 20 g castor sugar and whisk until stiff.

Fold one-third of the egg white mixture into the almond mixture. Then gradually fold in the remainder.

Fill muffin pans evenly with the mixture and level surfaces with a teaspoon.

Bake in preheated oven at 175°C for 20–25 minutes until golden brown. The cakes will slightly leave the sides of the pan.

Cool in pan before taking out. Remove lining paper and place cakes in cupcake cases. Drizzle ½ Tbsp fresh pineapple or orange juice into each cake. Top each with 2 pineapple wedges and a disc of kiwi fruit.

Place cold whipping cream in a well-chilled bowl or jug and whisk until firm peaks form. Fill a piping bag attached with a leaf-nozzle and pipe around the edges of the cakes, exposing fruits in the centre.

Refrigerate cakes and serve chilled.

Makes 12 cupcakes

Lemon Semolina Pear Sponge Cupcake

A flourless nutty light sponge cake with pears. Choose ripe but not mushy pears.

Eggs	**3, large (70 g each), separated**
Castor sugar	**110 g**
Grated lemon rind	**From 1 lemon**
Lemon juice	**1 Tbsp**
Semolina	**60 g**
Ground almonds	**35 g**
Ripe pear	**1 (approximately 185 g weight), peeled, cored and cut into 0.5-cm cubes of net weight 140 g**

Topping

Crushed almond flakes	**2 Tbsp (optional)**
Icing sugar to dust	
Large paper cases	**14 (5 cm base x 3.5 cm height)**

Line muffin pans with paper cases.

Place egg yolks in bowl of an electric cake mixer fitted with a balloon whisk and beat for 1 minute, adding sugar gradually.

Put in lemon rind and lemon juice and continue to beat until light, pale and thick and mixture leaves a trail when lifted.

Combine semolina and ground almonds. Fold in combined mixture. Leave mixture for 3 minutes to soften semolina.

Whisk egg whites in a separate bowl until soft peaks form. Fold into main mixture, one-third at a time, using a large metal spoon and taking care not to deflate the main mixture.

Spoon half of mixture to fill prepared cases. Gently level the surfaces and sprinkle over some pear cubes. Cover the pears with remaining mixture and level surfaces with a teaspoon. If desired, sprinkle over some crushed almond flakes.

Bake in preheated oven at 175°C for 20 minutes or until cakes are golden brown.

Cool cakes in pan before removing and dust with icing sugar.

Makes 14 cupcakes

Note: A balloon whisk gives excellent volume when beating egg whites or egg yolks. When whisking egg whites, ensure that the bowl is clean with no grease. The egg whites should not contain any droplets of egg yolk as this will prevent the beaten whites from standing in peaks.

Orange Sponge Cupcake with Orange Feather Icing

A fascinating mix of citrus and chocolate flavours suitable for entertaining during afternoon teas.

Plain (all-purpose) flour	50 g
Baking powder	$^1/_2$ tsp
Eggs	2, large (70–75 g each), separated
Castor sugar	50 g, reserve 1 Tbsp for whisking egg whites
Orange juice	1 Tbsp
Orange Feather Icing	
Icing sugar	150 g, sifted
Fresh orange juice	2 Tbsp, heated until hot
Topping	
Dark chocolate	35 g, melted
Medium paper cases	10 (4.5 cm base x 2.5 cm height)

Grease sides and line bases of 10 muffin pans with non-stick paper.

Sift plain flour and baking powder together.

Place egg whites in a mixing bowl and whisk with an electric hand-held rotary whisk until frothy. Beat in 1 Tbsp of sugar until stiff.

Place egg yolks in a separate bowl and beat till frothy. Add castor sugar and orange juice and beat until mixture is pale and thickened and leaves a trail when lifted.

Carefully fold egg yolk mixture into egg white mixture. Fold in sifted ingredients.

Spoon mixture evenly into prepared muffin pans. Level surfaces with a teaspoon.

Bake in preheated oven at 175°C for 15 minutes until pale golden and cooked through.

Cool in pan before turning out. Remove lining paper and place cakes in medium cupcake cases.

Prepare orange feather icing by heating orange juice in a microwave oven on high for 30 seconds. Gradually beat orange juice into icing sugar in a bowl until it is a thick creamy consistency. Spread icing on cupcakes.

Fill a piping bag fitted with a plain writing nozzle with melted chocolate and pipe four lines across icing on cake. Run pointed end of a skewer across the lines about 1 cm apart to form feathered lines. Do this quickly before icing sets.

Makes 10 cupcakes

Note: Both the orange icing and melted chocolate will set quickly. Prepare them only when you are ready to ice the cake. The orange icing and melted chocolate have to be soft when you run the skewer across them.

Cakes are best eaten the day they are made. If keeping for a couple of days, drizzle 2 extra tsp fresh orange juice onto each cake before icing.

Durian Dream Cupcake

Durians add a very Asian twist to this cupcake, giving it a rich and unique flavour.

Plain (all-purpose) flour	**50 g**
Baking powder	**¹/₂ tsp**
Eggs	**2, large (70–75 g each)**
Castor sugar	**50 g, reserve 1 Tbsp for whipping egg whites**
Water	**¹/₂ Tbsp**
Durian Cream Topping	
Durian pulp	**150 g**
Chilled whipping cream	**150 ml**
Topping	
Almond flakes	**15 g, toasted**
Large paper cases	**12 (6 cm base x 3.5 cm height)**

Grease sides and line bases of a 12-hole muffin pan with non-stick paper.

Sift plain flour and baking powder together.

Place egg whites in a deep bowl and whisk with a hand-held whisk until frothy. Beat in 1 Tbsp of the sugar until just stiff.

In a separate bowl, whisk the egg yolks until frothy. Add remaining sugar and water and whisk until pale and thickened.

Carefully fold the egg yolk mixture into the egg white mixture, one-third at a time. Fold in sifted ingredients.

Spoon mixture evenly to fill muffin pans and level surfaces with a teaspoon

Bake in preheated oven at 175°C for 15 minutes until golden brown and the cakes begin to leave the sides of the pan.

Cool in pan before turning out. Remove lining paper and place cakes in paper cases.

To make durian cream topping, place durian pulp in a small food processor and blend into a smooth puree. Refrigerate while preparing cream.

Whisk the cream in a well-chilled bowl until just stiff. Fold in chilled durian puree.

Fill a piping bag attached with a large star nozzle with the durian cream and pipe rosettes on each cupcake. Sprinkle surface with toasted almond flakes.

Refrigerate cupcakes and serve chilled.

Makes 12 cupcakes

Note: Choose good quality ripe durians for making the durian cream. The durian flesh should not be wet and runny. The durian cupcakes will keep well in a covered container in the refrigerator for 3–4 days.

Pandan Chiffon Cupcakes

This light and fluffy pandan cake will tantalise your tastebuds.

Plain (all-purpose) flour	75 g
Baking powder	$^1/_4$ tsp
Eggs	3, large (70–75 g each), separated
Cream of tartar	$^1/_8$ tsp
Castor sugar	65 g
Coconut cream (*pati santan*)	25 ml
Pandan juice	35 ml, strained
Condensed milk	1 Tbsp
Sunflower oil	1 Tbsp
Deep patty tins	18 (5.25 cm base x 3.5 cm height)
Medium paper cases	18

Grease sides and line bases of the patty tins with rounds of non-stick paper.

Sift plain flour and baking powder together.

Place egg whites and cream of tartar in a large bowl. Use an electric hand-held whisk and beat until frothy.

Gradually add sugar and continue to beat until just stiff.

In a separate bowl, whisk the egg yolks lightly with a fork. Then gradually beat into egg white mixture.

Combine coconut cream, pandan juice, condensed milk and sunflower oil.

Beat in combined liquid ingredients, by steadily pouring the liquid in and beating at the same time. Fold in sifted ingredients in two batches.

Spoon mixture into prepared tins.

Bake in preheated oven at 175°C for 15 minutes until golden brown.

Cool cakes, remove paper lining and turn cakes into paper cases.

Dust with icing sugar before serving.

Makes 18 cupcakes

Note: Coconut cream or *pati santan* is pure coconut milk obtained from squeezing grated coconut without adding water.

To obtain pandan juice, cut 3–4 *pandan* leaves into small pieces. Place in a blender with 60 ml water. Blend into a fine pulp. Strain and measure out required amount.

Eggs	2, large (70 g each), separated
Icing sugar	55 g, sifted
Dried white breadcrumbs	¹/₂ Tbsp (5 g)
Instant coffee powder	¹/₂ Tbsp
Cocoa powder	¹/₂ Tbsp (4 g), sifted
Walnuts	85 g, finely chopped

Coffee Cream

Cold butter	55 g, diced
Icing sugar	45 g, sifted
Cold evaporated milk	1 Tbsp
Instant coffee powder	1 ¹/₂ tsp

Chocolate rice or shavings for decoration	
Medium paper cases	8

Walnut Sponge Cupcake with Coffee Cream

An easy-to-do teatime flourless favourite.

Grease sides and line bases of 8 muffin pans with non-stick paper.

In a small deep bowl, whisk the egg yolks with an electric rotary whisk until frothy. Beat in the icing sugar until pale and thick.

Combine breadcrumbs and coffee powder and carefully fold into the mixture, followed by the cocoa powder. Stir in walnuts.

In a separate bowl, whisk egg whites until just stiff. Fold into egg yolk mixture, half at a time.

Spoon mixture evenly into prepared muffin pans and level surfaces with a teaspoon.

Bake in preheated oven at 175°C for 20 minutes or until well risen and a skewer inserted into the centre comes out clean.

Cool cakes in the pans. Remove cakes and peel off base lining paper and place into medium paper cases.

Spread or pipe coffee cream to cover cakes and sprinkle on top with chocolate rice or shavings.

* To Prepare Coffee Cream

In a small deep bowl, cream the butter and icing sugar until light and creamy. Beat in milk and coffee powder.

Makes 8 cupcakes

Note: To keep the cake mixture light, beat the egg yolks and sugar until light and airy. The breadcrumbs and coffee powder should not be granular. Pound them in a mortar and pestle into powder form. The walnuts have to be finely chopped. Do not pound them as oil will ooze out and form clumps.

You can make your own breadcrumbs by drying a couple of crustless white bread slices in the sun. Or place them in the oven to dry with the oven switched off after baking a batch of cakes. The breadcrumbs can then be grounded in an electric coffee grinder or small food chopper. They can be stored in airtight containers in the refrigerator for a few months.

Lemon Sponge Cupcakes with Grilled Caramel Topping

A refreshing cupcake with rice crispies, cherries and almond topping that will be a definite favourite with the young ones.

Plain (all-purpose) flour	75 g
Baking powder	³/₄ tsp
Egg	1, large (70–75 g)
Castor sugar	90 g
Lemon essence	¹/₄ tsp
Low-fat milk	1 Tbsp
Butter	60 g, melted and cooled
Lemon juice	1 Tbsp, combined with 1 Tbsp water, for sprinkling

Caramel Topping

Butter	30 g
Milk	1 Tbsp
Brown sugar	60 g
Almond slices	30 g, crushed
Glace cherries	20 g, rinsed and chopped
Rice crispies	20 g
Lemon juice	¹/₂ Tbsp
Large paper cases	10 (4.5 cm base x 3.5 cm height)

Line muffin pans with paper cases.

Sift plain flour and baking powder together.

Use a hand-held electric whisk to beat the egg and sugar until pale and thick. Gently fold in sifted ingredients and essence.

Set mixer on lowest speed, and mix in milk and melted butter until well combined.

Spoon mixture evenly into prepared cases and level surfaces with a teaspoon.

Bake in preheated oven at 175°C for 20 minutes or until a skewer inserted into centre of cakes comes out clean.

Remove from oven and drizzle a teaspoon of lemon juice mixture into each cake.

Spoon caramel topping onto cakes and spread to cover top of cakes.

Place in preheated grill at 175°C for 2–3 minutes until topping is just golden in colour.

Cool cakes in pan before removing.

* To Make Caramel Topping

Place butter and brown sugar in a small saucepan over low heat and stir until butter melts. Stir in nuts, cherries, rice crispies and lemon juice. Use immediately to cover cakes.

Makes 10 cupcakes

Note: The cake batter will only fill up to less than half of the paper cases. Do not worry about this as the batter will rise quite dramatically to almost above three-quarters level with enough space left to hold the topping.

Yoghurt Cupcakes

Apricot Yoghurt Cupcakes

This irresistibly rich apricot yoghurt cake has a citrusy taste from the orange and lemon rinds.

Self-raising flour	**110 g**
Baking powder	**1 tsp**
Castor sugar	**110 g**
Soft margarine or butter	**110 g, at room temperature**
Grated lemon rind	**From 1 lemon**
Grated orange rind	**From 1 orange**
Eggs	**2, large (70 g each), beaten**
Yoghurt or milk	**1 dsp**
Apricots	**60 g, chopped**

Topping
Almond flakes

Medium paper cases	**14 (4.5 cm x 2.5 cm height)**

Line 14 patty tins with paper cup cases.

Sift flour and baking powder into mixing bowl. Stir in castor sugar, margarine or butter, grated rinds, beaten eggs and yoghurt or milk.

Turn mixer on medium speed and beat for 2 minutes. Stir in apricots.

Fill paper cases up to three-quarters full. Sprinkle flaked almonds over top of cake.

Bake in preheated oven at 175°C for 20 minutes until golden and cooked through.

Makes 14 cupcakes

Chocolate Yoghurt Cupcake with Chocolate Cream

A double dose of chocolate is sure to leave you drooling for more.

Plain (all-pupose) flour	**125 g**
Baking powder	**¹/₄ tsp**
Bicarbonate of soda	**¹/₄ tsp**
Butter	**60 g**
Castor sugar	**110 g**
Dark chocolate	**60 g, melted and cooled**
Eggs	**2, large (70 g each)**
Salt	**A pinch**
Natural yoghurt	**75 ml**
Milk	**35 ml**
Vanilla essence	**¹/₂ tsp**

Chocolate Cream

Bittersweet chocolate	**100 g**
Butter	**25 g**
Whipping cream	**2 Tbsp**

Topping

Shredded coconut for sprinkling	

Large paper cases	**10 (5.5 cm base x 3.5 cm height)**

Line muffin pan with paper cases.

Sift plain flour, baking powder and bicarbonate soda together.

Cream butter and castor sugar until pale. Beat in melted chocolate and eggs, one at a time. Fold in sifted ingredients and salt.

Combine the yoghurt, milk and vanilla essence and stir into the chocolate mixture until well combined.

Fill the paper cases evenly with the mixture up to two-thirds full and level surfaces with a teaspoon

Bake in preheated oven at 175°C for 20 minutes or until well risen and firm to the touch when pressed lightly with a finger. Cool cakes in the pan.

Meanwhile, make chocolate cream by melting chocolate and butter in a heatproof bowl over gently boiling water until just melted. Cool slightly and stir in cream.

Spoon and spread the chocolate cream along the circumference of the cakes and sprinkle shredded coconut around the top of cakes.

Makes 10 cupcakes

Yoghurt Spice Cupcake

A spicy yoghurt cake that is easy to whip up.

Fresh white breadcrumbs	**20 g**
Walnuts	**20 g, coarsely chopped**
Self-raising flour	**110 g**
Ground cinnamon	**1 tsp**
Ground ginger	**$^1/_2$ tsp**
Ground cloves	**A pinch**
Butter	**65 g**
Soft brown sugar	**110 g,**
Eggs	**2, medium (65 g each), beaten with a fork**
Natural yoghurt	**80 ml**
Dark chocolate	**75 g, melted (optional)**
Large paper cases	**10 (5.5 cm base x 3.5 cm height)**

Spray 10 muffin pans with oil or grease with butter.

Combine the breadcrumbs and walnuts and mix well. Spoon a teaspoonful of the mixture onto the base of each muffin pan. Spread evenly to cover the base.

Sift self-raising flour, cinnamon, ginger and cloves together.

Cream the butter and sugar until well combined. Beat in the eggs, a little at a time to prevent curdling.

Fold in the sifted ingredients alternately with the yoghurt.

Fill the muffin pans evenly with the mixture up to two-thirds full and level surfaces with tthe back of a teaspoon.

Bake in preheated oven at 175°C for 20 minutes or until well risen and firm to the touch when pressed lightly with a finger.

Remove from oven and cool cakes in the pan for 10 minutes before turning out onto a wire rack to cool completely.

Place base up on white paper cases.

If desired, decorate with melted chocolate. Fill a piping bag with melted chocolate, snip a little off the end and pipe a spiral pattern on the breadcrumb and nut mixture surface.

Makes 10 cupcakes

Mocha Yoghurt Cupcake

Fragrant with chocolate and coffee, this light soft cake with an irresistible mocha icing and refreshing fruity topping is perfect for after-dinner dessert.

Self-raising flour	60 g
Cocoa powder	15 g
Butter	95 g, diced
Castor sugar	100 g
Vanilla essence	1 tsp
Eggs	2, large (70 g each), separated
Natural yoghurt	85 ml
Instant coffee powder	$^1/_2$ Tbsp, dissolved in $^1/_2$ Tbsp hot water and cooled

Mocha Chocolate Icing

Dark chocolate	60 g, chopped
Butter	30 g
Finely ground instant coffee powder	$^1/_2$ tsp
Icing sugar	20 g, sifted

Topping

Fresh mangosteen or mandarin orange segments for decoration

Medium paper cases   9

Line base of 9 muffin pans with non-stick paper. Grease or spray the sides of pans with oil.

Sift self-raising flour and cocoa powder together.

Cream butter, sugar and essence until light and fluffy. Beat in egg yolks, one at a time until well combined.

Fold in sifted ingredients alternately with yoghurt. Stir in cooled coffee mixture.

Whisk the egg whites until soft peaks form. Lightly fold through cake mixture in two batches.

Fill muffin pans up to half-full and level surfaces with the back of a teaspoon.

Bake in preheated oven at 175°C for 20 minutes or until well-risen and firm to the touch when pressed lightly with a finger.

Cool cakes in the pan before turning out onto a wire rack.

Remove lining paper and place each cake in a paper case. Cover with mocha chocolate icing. Top with fresh fruits.

To make mocha chocolate icing, place all the ingredients except icing sugar in a small saucepan. Stir over gentle heat until chocolate and butter melt. Stir in icing sugar without boiling until smooth. Use immediately.

Makes 9 cupcakes

Coconut Yoghurt Cupcake with Meringue Topping

A lovely cake with a contrast of textures.

Butter	**65 g**
Castor sugar	**60 g**
Egg	**1, large (70 g)**
Fresh grated or desiccated coconut	**20 g**
Vanilla essence	**$^1/_2$ tsp**
Yoghurt	**120 g**
Self-raising flour	**90 g, sifted**

Meringue Topping	
Egg white	**1 (40 g)**
Vanilla essence	**$^1/_4$ tsp**
Icing sugar	**90 g**
Desiccated coconut	**60 g**
Candied coconut for decoration	

Large paper cases	**9 (5.5 cm base x 3.5 cm height)**

Line muffin pans with paper cases.

Cream butter and sugar until light and creamy. Beat in egg for 1 minute. Stir in coconut and vanilla essence.

Beat in yoghurt until just combined. Fold in sifted flour.

Spoon mixture evenly into paper cases.

Bake in preheated oven at 175°C for 15 minutes or until just cooked through when tested with a wooden skewer.

Meanwhile, prepare meringue topping. Whisk egg white in a clean mixing bowl until fairly stiff. Add essence and beat in the icing sugar and desiccated coconut.

Remove cakes from the oven and spoon meringue topping on top of the cakes. Continue to bake for a further 15 minutes or until meringue topping is formed and turns light golden in colour.

Cool cakes in the pan. Remove and top each with candied coconut.

Makes 9 cupcakes

Lemon Yoghurt Cupcake with Lemon Syrup

This simple cake is always popular.

Hi-ratio flour	120 g
Baking powder	1 tsp
Butter	125 g, diced
Castor sugar	90 g, divided into 2 portions
Grated lemon rind	1 tsp
Lemon juice	$^1/_2$ Tbsp
Yoghurt	75 ml
Vanilla essence	$^1/_2$ tsp
Almonds	60 g, blanched and coarsely chopped
Egg whites	3, large (approximately 125 g)

Lemon Syrup

Lemon juice	2 Tbsp
Water	2 Tbsp
Dark brown or muscovado sugar	60 g

Topping

Almond nips for sprinkling	
Large paper cases	14 (4.5 cm x 3.5 height)

Line muffin pan with paper cup cases.

Sift hi-ratio flour and baking powder together.

Cream butter with half of the castor sugar until light and fluffy. Beat in lemon rind and juice, yoghurt and essence.

Fold in sifted ingredients and the almonds.

Whisk egg whites with remaining sugar, in a separate bowl, until soft peaks form. Fold into main mixture, one-third at a time.

Spoon mixture evenly into prepared cases and level surfaces with a teaspoon. Top each with an almond.

Bake in preheated oven at 175°C for 20–22 minutes or until just cooked through.

Combine lemon syrup ingredients and warm slightly to melt sugar. Remove cakes from oven and drizzle a dessertspoon of lemon syrup into each cake.

Leave until cold and for the syrup to soak into the cakes. Sprinkle with almond nips.

Makes 14 cupcakes

Note: These tangy lemony cupcakes are a great way to make use of leftover egg whites. Egg whites will keep for several days in the refrigerator and for a couple of months in the freezer. The best way to freeze egg white is to use an ice-cube tray, one egg white in each compartment. You can then easily keep track of the number of egg whites stored.

Pistachio Yoghurt Cupcake

A healthy choice of light spongy and moist cupcake, if you replace melted butter with sunflower oil. Pistachios are packed with nutrients and fibre. It is a good source of vitamin B-6, thiamine, phosphorus, magnesium and copper. This nut is cholesterol-free and contains mostly monounsaturated fat.

Self-raising flour	**75 g**
Baking powder	**$^1/_2$ tsp**
Unsalted pistachios	**60 g**
Eggs	**3, large (70 g each), separated**
Castor sugar	**110 g, divided into 2 equal portions**
Yoghurt	**90 ml**
Butter	**60 g, melted and cooled**
Salt	**A pinch**
Pistachios	**20 g, coarsely chopped for topping**
Icing sugar for dusting	
Large paper cases	**14 (5 cm base x 5 cm height)**

Line muffin pans with paper cases.

Place pistachios in a pepper grinder or small food processor and grind until fine.

Sift self-raising flour and baking powder together.

Put egg yolks in a small bowl with half of the sugar and whisk with a hand-held electric whisk until pale and very thick.

Mix in yoghurt and melted butter. Fold in pistachios, sifted ingredients and salt.

In a separate bowl, whisk the egg whites until soft peaks form. Beat in remaining sugar and continue beating until just stiff.

Gently fold in the egg white mixture, one-third at a time into the pistachio mixture.

Use a large ice-cream scoop to fill the paper cases evenly with the mixture up to two-thirds full and level surfaces with the back of a teaspoon. Sprinkle with chopped pistachios.

Bake in preheated oven at 175°C for 23–25 minutes or until top is golden brown.

Remove and cool cupcakes in the pan. Dust with icing sugar, if preferred.

Makes 14 cupcakes

Stem ginger

Young ginger	**1 kg, skinned and cut into 2-cm cubes**
Sugar	**900 g (4 cups)**
Water	**900 ml (4 cups)**

Immerse ginger in cold water and let stand for 2 hours. Drain. Place ginger in a heatproof dish and add enough water to cover ginger completely. Boil rapidly, uncovered, for 5 minutes. Drain.

Return ginger to heatproof dish and add water to cover ginger completely. Bring to the boil, lower heat, and simmer covered for 45 minutes or until ginger is just tender. Drain.

Add 450 g (2 cups) of sugar to 900 ml water and stir over low heat until sugar is dissolved. Add sugar water to drained ginger, bring to the boil, reduce heat and simmer covered for 10 minutes.

Remove from heat, leave to cool and allow to stand for 24 hours. Remove ginger from syrup and set aside.

Add 1 cup sugar to syrup and bring to a boil. Simmer uncovered for 5 minutes until sugar is dissolved. Pour over ginger and leave to stand for 24 hours.

Repeat process with remaining cup of sugar.

Praline

Sugar	**200 g**
Water	**85 ml**
Walnuts or pecan nuts	**30 g, finely chopped**

To prepare praline, line a 28-cm square cookie tray with foil. Foil should come up to the sides of the pan. Lightly grease the foil with butter or margarine. Set aside.

Put the sugar and water into a thick base saucepan and heat gently until the sugar dissolves. If the sugar starts to crystallise on the sides, brush the crystals down with a damp pastry brush. Cook without stirring until the sugar turns golden.

Pour syrup over foil-lined tray. Tilt the tray so that the syrup forms a thin layer and quickly sprinkle walnuts over and set aside to harden.

Lift the praline from the foil and break into pieces by pressing with your hand. It will shatter into small and large pieces. Use the smaller ones on the edges or centre of the cake.

Marzipan

Icing sugar	**125 g, sifted**
Castor sugar	**125 g**
Ground almonds	**225 g**
Egg	**1, small, lightly beaten**
Lemon juice	**½ tsp**
Almond essence	**A few drops**

Put sugars and almond into bowl of food processor. Mix for a few seconds. Add remaining ingredients and pulse to form a crumbly dough. Remove blade and pour into a mixing bowl. Knead into a stiff paste. Place in plastic bag and refrigerate overnight before use.

Note: Commercial marzipan or almond paste is easily available in leading supermarkets but it is far cheaper to make your own. It can be used as a coating for cakes to provide a smooth surface for royal icing and to prevent fruit cakes from discolouring icing. You can also colour and shape them into fruits and vegetables for use as decoration, e.g. making baby carrots for the Carrot and Pineapple Cupcakes. Marzipan can be kept frozen for up to one month.

Candied Orange Slices

Oranges	**2, small to medium, sliced crosswise into 0.4-cm slices**
Water	**¾ cup (175 ml)**
Sugar	**275 g**

Place orange slices (or orange peel florets or orange strips) in a medium saucepan. Cover the oranges with water and bring to the boil. Drain and repeat procedure. Drain and set aside.

Place sugar and water in a non-stick saucepan and stir over low heat to dissolve sugar. Add oranges and bring to a slow boil.

Reduce heat to low and simmer, uncovered, for about 20 minutes or until syrup is thick. Cool syrup and oranges.

Stack orange slices carefully to retain their shape in an airtight container. Pour in the syrup. Cover and store in the refrigerator.

Weights and Measures

Quantities for this book are given in Metric and American (spoon and cup) measures. Standard spoon and cup measurements used are: 1 tsp = 5 ml, 1 Tbsp = 15 ml, 1 cup = 250 ml. All measures are level unless otherwise stated.

LIQUID AND VOLUME MEASURES

Metric	Imperial	American
5 ml	$1/6$ fl oz	1 teaspoon
10 ml	$1/3$ fl oz	1 dessertspoon
15 ml	$1/2$ fl oz	1 tablespoon
60 ml	2 fl oz	$1/4$ cup (4 tablespoons)
85 ml	$2^1/2$ fl oz	$1/3$ cup
90 ml	3 fl oz	$3/8$ cup (6 tablespoons)
125 ml	4 fl oz	$1/2$ cup
180 ml	6 fl oz	$3/4$ cup
250 ml	8 fl oz	1 cup
300 ml	10 fl oz ($1/2$ pint)	$1^1/4$ cups
375 ml	12 fl oz	$1^1/2$ cups
435 ml	14 fl oz	$1^3/4$ cups
500 ml	16 fl oz	2 cups
625 ml	20 fl oz (1 pint)	$2^1/2$ cups
750 ml	24 fl oz ($1^1/5$ pints)	3 cups
1 litre	32 fl oz ($1^3/5$ pints)	4 cups
1.25 litres	40 fl oz (2 pints)	5 cups
1.5 litres	48 fl oz ($2^2/5$ pints)	6 cups
2.5 litres	80 fl oz (4 pints)	10 cups

DRY MEASURES

Metric	Imperial
30 grams	1 ounce
45 grams	$1^1/2$ ounces
55 grams	2 ounces
70 grams	$2^1/2$ ounces
85 grams	3 ounces
100 grams	$3^1/2$ ounces
110 grams	4 ounces
125 grams	$4^1/2$ ounces
140 grams	5 ounces
280 grams	10 ounces
450 grams	16 ounces (1 pound)
500 grams	1 pound, $1^1/2$ ounces
700 grams	$1^1/2$ pounds
800 grams	$1^3/4$ pounds
1 kilogram	2 pounds, 3 ounces
1.5 kilograms	3 pounds, $4^1/2$ ounces
2 kilograms	4 pounds, 6 ounces

LENGTH

Metric	Imperial
0.5 cm	$1/4$ inch
1 cm	$1/2$ inch
1.5 cm	$3/4$ inch
2.5 cm	1 inch

OVEN TEMPERATURE

	°C	°F	Gas Regulo
Very slow	120	250	1
Slow	150	300	2
Moderately slow	160	325	3
Moderate	180	350	4
Moderately hot	190/200	370/400	5/6
Hot	210/220	410/440	6/7
Very hot	230	450	8
Super hot	250/290	475/550	9/10

ABBREVIATION

tsp	teaspoon
Tbsp	tablespoon
g	gram
kg	kilogram
ml	millilitre